At Issue

| Pandemics

Other Books in the At Issue Series:

Are Textbooks Biased?

Book Banning

The BP Oil Spill

Can Diets Be Harmful?

Cyberbullying

DNA Databases

The Ethics of Capital Punishment

How Does Advertising Impact Teen Behavior?

Human Waste

Identity Theft

Rebuilding the World Trade Center Site

Should Music Lyrics Be Censored?

Space Exploration

Student Loans

Weapons of War

What Is the Impact of E-Waste?

At Issue

|Pandemics

Jacqueline Langwith, Book Editor

GREENHAVEN PRESS
A part of Gale, Cengage Learning

GALE
CENGAGE Learning·

Detroit • New York • San Francisco • New Haven, Conn • Waterville, Maine • London

Elizabeth Des Chenes, *Managing Editor*

For more information, contact:
Greenhaven Press
27500 Drake Rd.
Farmington Hills, MI 48331-3535
Or you can visit our Internet site at gale.cengage.com

Articles in Greenhaven Press anthologies are often edited for length to meet page requirements. In addition, original titles of these works are changed to clearly present the main thesis and to explicitly indicate the author's opinion. Every effort is made to ensure that Greenhaven Press accurately reflects the original intent of the authors. Every effort has been made to trace the owners of copyrighted material.

Cover image copyright © Images.com/Corbis.

LIBRARY OF CONGRESS CATALOGING-IN-PUBLICATION DATA

Pandemics / Jacqueline Langwith, editor.
    p. cm. -- (At issue)
Summary: "Pandemics: Pandemic Preparedness Is a Matter of National Security; Pandemic Preparedness Is a Public Health Matter; Pandemic Preparedness Should Include Quarantines And Other Interventions; Pandemic Preparedness Planning Requires A Global Response; International Pandemic Response Is an Excuse to Globalize the Planet; The World Must Ensure There Is Equal Access to Pandemic Vaccines; Negotiating Equitable Access to Pandemic Vaccines Will Be Difficult; A Universal Flu Vaccine Could Protect Against A Pandemic; The 2009 Swine Flu Pandemic Was Exaggerated By the World Health Organization; The WHO Had No Agenda Regarding the Swine Flu Pandemic; The Virus That Caused The 2009 Pandemic Will Likely Die Out; There Will Be Another Pandemic"-- Provided by publisher.
    Includes bibliographical references and index.
    ISBN 978-0-7377-5588-6 (hardback) -- ISBN 978-0-7377-5589-3 (paperback)
    1. Epidemics--Juvenile literature. I. Langwith, Jacqueline.
    RA653.5.P368 2011
    614.4--dc23
                                                            2011029279

Printed in the United States of America
1 2 3 4 5 6 7 15 14 13 12 11

Contents

Introduction   7

1. Pandemic Preparedness Is a Matter   11
   of National Security
   Scott Gottlieb

2. Pandemic Preparedness Is a Public   16
   Health Matter
   *George J. Annas, Wendy K. Mariner,
   and Wendy E. Parmet*

3. Pandemic Preparedness Should Include   22
   Quarantines and Other Interventions
   Alexandra Minna Stern and Howard Markel

4. Pandemic Preparedness Planning Requires   30
   a Global Response
   Harvey Rubin and C. Kameswara Rao

5. An International Pandemic Response   39
   Is an Excuse to Globalize the Planet
   Jon Rappoport

6. The World Must Ensure Equal Access   52
   to Pandemic Flu Vaccines
   Tadataka Yamada

7. Negotiating Equal Access to Pandemic   57
   Flu Vaccines Will Be Difficult
   David P. Fidler

8. A Universal Flu Vaccine Could Preempt   67
   a Pandemic
   Kelly Morris

9. The World Health Organization Exaggerated   73
   the 2009 Swine Flu Pandemic
   Michael Fumento

10. The World Health Organization Handled the 2009 Swine Flu Pandemic Well 77
World Health Organization

11. Another Pandemic Is Inevitable 81
John M. Barry

Organizations to Contact 87

Bibliography 93

Index 98

Introduction

"In health care, as elsewhere, scarcity is the mother of allocation."

—Bioethicists Govind Persad, Alan Wertheimer, and Ezekiel J. Emanuel

A twenty-four-year-old pregnant woman, a thirty-three-year-old mother and her nine-month-old baby, a seventy-six-year-old grandfather and his twelve-year-old grandson, a fifty-year-old autoworker with heart disease, and a healthy forty-year-old stock broker are all standing in a hypothetical line waiting for a pandemic flu vaccine. There are seven of them, but only enough vaccine for four of them. The vaccine has already been diluted as much as possible to spread it out among as many people as possible. You are the director of the public health facility they have all come to hoping to get vaccinated for a lethal influenza pandemic spreading throughout the United States. You must decide who gets the four doses of the vaccine and who must get sent away without it. This is a hypothetical scenario, but it illustrates one of many difficult decisions that public health officials could face if a lethal influenza pandemic spreads throughout the country. Vaccine distribution during an influenza pandemic differs from the distribution of the seasonal flu vaccine and poses unique challenges for public health officials.

Each year, the seasonal flu vaccine is developed, manufactured, and distributed, following a generally predictable pattern. Preparations for the seasonal flu vaccine begin early each year, as public health agencies in the United States and around the world collect the flu strains circulating in their geographic area and send them to one of five World Health Organization (WHO) laboratories. After the viruses are tested, the US Food and Drug Administration and WHO pick three strains of flu viruses to go into the seasonal flu vaccine for the fall and winter. It generally takes at least six months for manufacturers to make large quantities of the vaccine, so manufacturers start working right away so they can be ready to begin shipping the vaccine to clinics, doctors, and public health agencies beginning in August.

Vaccinating people during an influenza pandemic is much different than vaccinating people for the seasonal flu. Pandemic flu viruses are typically new strains that public health officials have not seen before and which are not covered by the seasonal flu vaccine. Vaccine manufacturers will have to shift gears from producing the seasonal flu and immediately begin working on a vaccine for the pandemic virus. No matter how hard or fast they work, it will still take months to produce enough vaccine to begin distributing it to the public. With no immunity in the population the virus will spread unhindered and likely cause significant mortality. When the vaccine manufacturers have finally produced enough vaccine to begin distributing it, there will not be nearly enough to protect everyone. The public will probably be scared, and demand for the vaccine will be overwhelming. Public health officials will be placed in the difficult position of deciding who should get the first doses of limited vaccine supplies.

According to guidelines issued by the US Department of Health and Human Services (DHHS) and the Department of Homeland Security (DHS) in 2009, people who serve important societal needs, such as military personnel, health care workers, and first responders, would be vaccinated before the general public. The departments considered it ethically appropriate to vaccinate these groups before the general public because many of the people in these groups assume increased risk of becoming infected because of their jobs, and these groups will help to minimize the impact of the pandemic on the general public.

When the vaccine becomes available to the general public, the DHHS/DHS generally prioritizes vaccine distribution based on age and health, with the intent of saving as many lives as possible. People who face the highest risk of dying from the pandemic flu because of age or medical condition are vaccinated first. In the hypothetical situation described above, the DHHS/DHS guidelines direct that the twenty-four-year-old pregnant woman would be the first person to receive the vaccine. She would be followed by the nine-month-old infant, the infant's thirty-three-year-old mother, the twelve-year-old boy, the fifty-year-old with heart disease, and then the grandfather in his seventies. The last person to receive the vaccine would be the healthy forty-year-old.

Some medical ethicists have proposed an alternative vaccine distribution formula that is based on the concept of "complete lives." In a January 2009 article published in the medical journal the *Lancet*, American bioethicists Govind Persad, Alan Wertheimer, and Ezekiel J. Emanuel asserted that using the "saving the most lives," principle to distribute vaccines during a pandemic is generally flawed. They believe that a life-cycle-allocation principle based on the idea that each person should have an opportunity to live through all the stages of life is more appropriate for a pandemic. Their complete lives system of distributing vaccine generally favors giving the vaccine to healthy individuals aged between roughly fifteen and forty years first. The complete lives system would mean that the thirty-three-year-old mother and forty-year-old stock broker would generally be the first to receive the vaccine.

Deciding who should be the first to receive a pandemic vaccine when supplies are limited is just one of many contentious issues associated with pandemics. Other contentious issues include, how pandemic vaccines should be distributed among different countries, the best way to prepare for a pandemic, and when a flu outbreak should be labeled a pandemic. In *At Issue: Pandemics*, public health experts, government officials, and journalists provide their opinions on these and other issues surrounding this serious public health threat.

1

Pandemic Preparedness Is a Matter of National Security

Scott Gottlieb

Scott Gottlieb, a resident fellow at the American Enterprise Institute and a practicing physician, has served at the US Food and Drug Administration and the Centers for Medicare and Medicaid Services.

The US government should view pandemic preparedness as a matter of national security, not solely as a public health challenge. When viewed as a security issue, it becomes imperative that the government take immediate steps to increase domestic vaccine-manufacturing capacity. This includes guaranteeing annual purchases of seasonal flu vaccine, reworking Food and Drug Administration regulations to allow expanded vaccine production, and investing in new vaccine technologies. Protecting the US population requires the US government to consider pandemic preparedness as a matter of national strategic planning.

Memories of 2009's scary emergence of H1N1 "swine flu" have faded along with new cases of the virus, but the episode is worth remembering for the weakness it exposed in our domestic security.

The [Barack] Obama administration has included $300 million for pandemic flu preparedness in its current [fiscal year 2011] budget, but that won't be enough to build even a single new vaccine manufacturing plant in the U.S. Yet the widespread shortage of swine flu shots last fall should have taught us the importance of a domestic capacity to produce pandemic vaccines as a matter of national strategic planning.

Pandemic preparedness should be viewed as a matter of our national security, not solely a public health challenge.

Our Vulnerability Exposed

The depth of our vulnerability was laid bare when two close allies—Australia and Canada—effectively nationalized their domestic flu vaccine plants, seizing H1N1 swine flu shots destined for the U.S. This is one of the reasons why America didn't have enough vaccine when we needed it.

In Australia, the government pressured vaccine maker CSL Limited to turn over 36 million doses of H1N1 vaccine contracted for by the U.S. and produced in an Australian-based manufacturing plant. Meanwhile, in Canada, where British drug maker GlaxoSmithKline maintains its U.S.-focused flu vaccine facility, the company had to assure the local government that Canadians would be served from that manufacturing plant before Americans could receive any of their vaccine orders.

Pandemic preparedness should be viewed as a matter of our national security, not solely a public health challenge, with an intensive effort to build domestic vaccine capacity to serve our population.

Surprisingly, there is only one full-scale facility on U.S. soil for producing flu vaccine (owned and operated by Sanofi Aventis). The other four companies licensed by the Food and Drug Administration [FDA] to produce flu vaccine all manufacture, fill and finish their shots in facilities located mostly in Europe. This leaves America at the mercy of foreign governments.

Even more worrisome, the single facility that the U.S. has on its soil won't help against the full range of potential pandemics. Our sole domestic facility relies on older-generation technology that uses chicken eggs as incubators to grow the vaccine components. While this is adequate for producing vaccine against a swine flu, if we're hit by avian "bird" flu, the egg process could be unfeasible. Bird flu can destroy the chickens and the eggs before vaccine components can be harvested. What's needed are manufacturing facilities that use cells as incubators for growing vaccines rather than chicken eggs.

H1N1 is arguably a milder flu, and a worse pandemic is inevitable. Imagine how other nations might behave when it strikes. Manufacturing sites would be seized—every country for itself.

Increasing US Vaccine Capacity

The Department of Health and Human Services gave contracts to five companies to build cell-based facilities several years ago. Two of the companies gave up and returned the money. Another two are building plants overseas. Only a single firm, Novartis, is building a full scale, cell-based plant in the U.S. It's been under construction for more than two years and won't be fully operational for about another four. It shows the long lead-time needed to create production capacity.

To protect Americans, the government should also guarantee the annual purchase of a certain amount of seasonal flu vaccine. This would enable the industry to reliably forecast demand, spurring investment in new facilities that could also be used to produce vaccine in a pandemic. The annual procurement should favor vaccines produced in U.S. plants and with newer, cell-based methods.

Purchased vaccine could be distributed domestically, or better still, donated to Asian nations such as Vietnam. Flu strains often originate in Asia and we rely on local Asian governments' to undertake vigorous surveillance and share emerging virus strains. Giving them free shots would encourage vaccination to reduce spread and give nations more skin in global efforts to stem outbreaks.

A stumbling block to more domestic vaccine capacity owes to how vaccines are regulated. The FDA often requires vaccine from each plant to be tested in completely separate clinical trials. There are good reasons why biologics such as vaccines can vary from one production run to the next. But these constraints make it far more economical for drug firms to expand existing vaccine facilities rather than build new ones. With better regulatory tools, there may be ways for FDA to allow a single clinical trial to suffice, even when similar vaccines are produced at two different sites.

Viewed as a problem of public health preparedness, our incremental pandemic preparations may seem adequate. Seen as a national security threat, it's clear that our current efforts are insufficient.

Finally, despite its benefits, cell culture is just a new way of making an old vaccine. What's really needed is technology that allows us to produce vaccine without culturing the flu virus itself.

New processes such as recombinant technologies allow the manufacture of small fragments of virus (called viruslike particles) rather than relying on whole copies of the bug. This and similar innovations can yield more vaccine in shorter time—about 10–12 weeks to scale up a big production run, compared with 26 weeks using an egg-based vaccine or 16 for a cell culture. The newer methods give us a better chance to intervene with vaccine during the first wave of a pandemic.

Given the long lead times to new medical products, if we're struck by another pandemic in 5 or 10 years, we'll be fighting it with whatever technology we invest in today. Viewed as a problem of public health preparedness, our incremental pandemic preparations may seem adequate. Seen as a national security threat, it's clear that our current efforts are insufficient.

2

Pandemic Preparedness Is a Public Health Matter

George J. Annas, Wendy K. Mariner, and Wendy E. Parmet

George J. Annas and Wendy K. Mariner are professors at Boston University School of Public Health, School of Law, and School of Medicine. Wendy E. Parmet is a professor at Northeastern University School of Law in Boston.

Many government policy makers have mistakenly embraced law enforcement and national security approaches to pandemic preparedness. History, however, has shown that these approaches are ineffective and dangerous. Forced vaccinations, quarantines, and other "liberty-limiting" measures breed public mistrust and can cause people to evade public health authorities. Pandemic preparedness requires a civil liberties–friendly, public health response that, among other things, emphasizes community engagement, protects minorities and the socially disadvantaged, and relies on voluntary measures.

The spread of a new, deadly strain of avian influenza has raised fears of a potential human pandemic. While the virus is not easily transmissible to humans, were it to mutate to be more highly contagious to or between humans—a possiblity whose probability is unknown—an influenza pandemic could occur.

Government agencies have an essential role to play in helping to prevent and mitigate epidemics. Unfortunately, in

George J. Annas, Wendy K. Mariner, and Wendy E. Parmet, "Executive Summary," *Pandemic Preparedness: The Need for a Public Health—Not a Law Enforcement/National Security—Approach*, American Civil Liberties Union, January 2008. Copyright © 2008 The American Civil Liberties Union. Reproduced by permission.

recent years, our government's approach to preparing the nation for a possible influenza pandemic has been highly misguided. Too often, policymakers are resorting to law enforcement and national security-oriented measures that not only suppress individual rights unnecessarily, but have proven to be ineffective in stopping the spread of disease and saving lives.

The following [viewpoint] examines the relationship between civil liberties and public health in contemporary U.S. pandemic planning and makes a series of recommendations for developing a more effective, civil liberties–friendly approach.

Rather than focusing on well-established measures for protecting the lives and health of Americans, policymakers have recently embraced an approach that views public health policy through the prism of national security and law enforcement. This model assumes that we must "trade liberty for security." As a result, instead of helping individuals and communities through education and provision of health care, today's pandemic prevention focuses on taking aggressive, coercive actions against those who are sick. People, rather than the disease, become the enemy.

American history contains vivid reminders that grafting the values of law enforcement and national security onto public health is both ineffective and dangerous.

Lessons from History

American history contains vivid reminders that grafting the values of law enforcement and national security onto public health is both ineffective and dangerous. Too often, fears aroused by disease and epidemics have justified abuses of state power. Highly discriminatory and forcible vaccination and quarantine measures adopted in response to outbreaks of the plague and smallpox over the past century have consistently accelerated rather than slowed the spread of disease, while fomenting public distrust and, in some cases, riots.

The lessons from history should be kept in mind whenever we are told by government officials that "tough," liberty-limiting actions are needed to protect us from dangerous diseases. Specifically:

- Coercion and brute force are rarely necessary. In fact they are generally counterproductive—they gratuitously breed public distrust and encourage the people who are most in need of care to evade public health authorities.

- On the other hand, effective, preventive strategies that rely on voluntary participation do work. Simply put, people do not *want* to contract smallpox, influenza or other dangerous diseases. They *want* positive government help in avoiding and treating disease. As long as public officials are working to help people rather than to punish them, people are likely to engage willingly in any and all efforts to keep their families and communities healthy.

- Minorities and other socially disadvantaged populations tend to bear the brunt of tough public health measures.

Post-9/11 Pandemic Plans

Current pandemic planning policies fail to heed history's lessons. Since 9/11, the [George W.] Bush Administration has adopted an all-hazards, one-size-fits-all approach to disaster planning. By assuming that the same preparedness model can be applied to any kind of disaster—whether biological, chemical, explosive, natural or nuclear—the all-hazards approach fails to take into account essential specifics of the nature of the virus or bacteria, how it is transmitted, and whether infection can be prevented or treated. Following this flawed logic, several state-based proposals have sought to address any "public health emergency," [and have] ignored effective steps that states could take to mitigate an epidemic, such as reinvigorating their public health infrastructure, and instead resorted to punitive, police-state tactics such as forced examinations, vaccination and treatment and criminal sanctions for those individuals who did not follow the rules.

Specific pandemic flu plans have also been adopted by the federal government and nearly every state and locality. The plans are poorly coordinated and dangerously counterproductive. By assuming the "worst case" scenario, all of the plans rely heavily on a punitive approach and emphasize extreme measures such as quarantine and forced treatment. For example, the U.S. Department of Health and Human Service's *Pandemic Influenza Plan* posits a "containment strategy" that calls for massive uses of government force, for example, to ban public gatherings, isolate symptomatic individuals, restrict the movement of individuals, or compel vaccination or treatment.

Toward a New Paradigm

This [viewpoint] calls for a new paradigm for pandemic preparedness based on the following general principles:

1. *Health*—The goal of preparing for a pandemic is to protect the lives and health of all people in America, not law enforcement or national security.

2. *Justice*—Preparation for a potential pandemic (or any disaster) should ensure a fair distribution of the benefits and burdens of precautions and responses and equal respect for the dignity and autonomy of each individual.

3. *Transparency*—Pandemic preparedness requires transparent communication of accurate information among all levels of government and the public in order to warrant public trust.

4. *Accountability*—Everyone, including private individuals and organizations and government agencies and officials, should be accountable for their actions before, during and after an emergency.

In addition, a number of specific recommendations are made for a sounder approach to pandemic preparedness that protects health while safeguarding liberty, privacy and democracy. These include the following:

- Stockpiling and ensuring fair and efficient distribution and rationing of vaccines and medication;

- Emphasizing community engagement rather than individual responsibility;

- Protecting minorities and socially disadvantaged individuals from discriminatory rationing schemes for vaccination and treatment or from bearing the burden of coercive health measures;

- Relying wherever possible on voluntary social distancing measures rather than mandatory quarantines;

- Providing counsel and procedural protections to those individuals proposed for detention or travel restrictions;

- Protecting individual privacy in disease surveillance and investigation; and

- Ensuring that public health actors remain accountable for their actions in accordance with the law.

The threat of a new pandemic will never subside. But the notion that we need to "trade liberty for security" is misguided and dangerous.

The threat of a new pandemic will never subside. But the notion that we need to "trade liberty for security" is misguided and dangerous. Public health concerns cannot be addressed with law enforcement or national security tools. If we allow the fear associated with a potential outbreak to justify the suspension of liberties in the name of public health, we risk not only undermining our fundamental rights, but alienating the very communities and individuals that are in need of help and thereby fomenting the spread of disease.

Maintaining fundamental freedoms is essential for encouraging public trust and cooperation. If our public agencies work hand in hand with communities to provide them with a healthy environment, access to care, and a means for protecting their families, rather than treating them as the enemy, we will be far better prepared for a potential outbreak.

3

Pandemic Preparedness Should Include Quarantines and Other Interventions

Alexandra Minna Stern and Howard Markel

Alexandra Minna Stern is the associate director of the Center for the History of Medicine, and an associate professor of obstetrics and gynecology, history, and American culture at the University of Michigan. Howard Markel is an internationally known scholar in pediatrics and the history of medicine, a member of the National Academy of Sciences, and the director of the Center for the History of Medicine at the University of Michigan. He has authored several books, including the award-winning Quarantine! *in 2003.*

Nonpharmaceutical interventions (NPIs), such as isolation, quarantines, and school closings are important tools that governments can use to contain a pandemic. History has shown that voluntary NPIs are the most effective, while mandatory NPIs are challenging because they may infringe on individual rights. If a pandemic becomes serious enough, however, mandatory NPIs may become necessary to prevent large-scale harm to the public. Lawmakers and policy makers should establish a framework for when voluntary and mandatory NPIs are necessary, and they should communicate this framework to the public.

Alexandra Minna Stern and Howard Markel, "Influenza Pandemic," *From Birth to Death and Bench to Clinic: The Hastings Center Bioethics Briefing Book for Journalists, Policymakers, and Campaigns,* edited by Mary Crowley, Garrison, NY: The Hastings Center, 2008, pp. 89–92. Copyright © 2008 The Hastings Center. Reproduced by permission.

If the United States is confronted with pandemic influenza, communities across the country will decide which nonpharmaceutical interventions (NPI), if any, to implement before adequate vaccine and antiviral supplies are developed and distributed. NPI encompass traditional public health strategies of isolation and quarantine, school closures, and social distancing measures such as gathering bans, the cancellation of public events, and restricted transportation. Two critical questions emerge from a potential pandemic scenario: Can communities apply NPI in a manner that maximizes the common good and minimizes negative social and economic consequences? What are the ethical implications of NPI, particularly when it comes to balancing individual liberties with the need to protect the public's health?

Voluntary and Mandatory NPI

The 1918–1919 influenza pandemic was the most deadly infectious calamity in human history. Approximately 40 million individuals died worldwide, including 550,000 individuals in the United States. During the 1918 pandemic, virtually every city in the United States and much of the world employed mandatory and voluntary NPI to mitigate the pandemic, making it especially tantalizing for policymakers to scour the historical record for counsel.

If we accept that a 1918-like influenza pandemic would necessitate a public health response, what criteria should we use to apply a menu of NPI that is ethical and efficacious? The historical record of past epidemics indicates that NPI work with the most benefit and least friction when they are voluntary, respect and rely on individual autonomy, and avoid the use of police powers. Furthermore, recent research indicates that the timing, duration, and choice of NPI played an important role in a community's overall pandemic outcome.

Past experiences with pandemic—even those as different as influenza in 1918 and SARS [severe acute respiratory syndrome] in 2003—teach us that voluntary NPI usually meet ethical criteria and often can work to empower individuals and communities to protect the public health. For example, studies of the 2003 SARS epidemic in Toronto, Canada, found that the majority of persons exposed to that virus voluntarily consented to home quarantine in order to protect the health of others. They reported "civic duty" as their primary motivation for home and work quarantine. Additionally, a 2006 Harvard School of Public Health survey found that most Americans, if confronted with pandemic influenza, would make major changes in their daily lives for up to one month to comply with recommended voluntary NPI. It is also striking that in 1918 in Chicago, one of just a handful of cities that did not order school closure, absenteeism rates neared 50% during the height of the epidemic. Of their own volition, many Americans in cities across the country sequestered themselves in their homes. Given that the 1918 pandemic coincided with a time of war and heightened patriotism, Americans were particularly inclined to heed governmental mandates. When the pandemic hit the United States in September 1918, the term "slacker," originally applied to those who refused to support the war effort, was quickly applied to people who protested public health edicts.

Yet even as public health officials can be heartened by evidence of ethically sound and voluntary NPI cooperation, as the severity of a pandemic increases, so too will the pressure on government to enact mandatory NPI in order to mitigate transmission and reduce the case fatality rate. In the Centers for Disease Control and Prevention's 2007 guidelines on community mitigation, mandatory measures are only recommended for pandemics whose case fatality ratio rises above one percent, which would rate them as category 4 or 5 in the Pandemic Severity Index (the 1918 flu pandemic was a category 5). Based on the 2006 U.S. population, this means that the projected deaths from pandemic influenza would have to surpass one million before mandatory measures would be recommended. Given such projections and the political and social imperatives to act in the event of a category 5 influenza pandemic, can mandatory NPI be applied in an ethical and transparent manner that inspires compliance?

Even as public health officials can be heartened by evidence of ethically sound and voluntary NPI cooperation, as the severity of a pandemic increases, so too will the pressure on government to enact mandatory NPI.

Considering Mandatory NPI

Mandatory NPI was widely used across the United States in the 1918 influenza pandemic. In several instances, removed communities such as islands (including American Samoa) took advantage of their geographical isolation to restrict access and thus shield themselves entirely from pandemic influenza. However, these success stories were the exception, not the rule. Indeed, many communities applied NPI in less than systematic fashion, ultimately experiencing problems of noncompliance and NPI fatigue, especially when orders were enacted, rescinded, and reenacted two or more times.

Some experts remain so concerned about the secondary and unintended consequences of NPI that they refrain from recommending any course of action in the event of pandemic influenza. Yet such reticence runs contrary to the mission of public health and the common sense compulsion to act in the face of potential death or destruction. In ethical terms, inaction can carry serious problems, in this case by violating the harm principle (which maintains that individual autonomy can be curtailed rightfully in order to prevent harm and injury to others) and disregarding escalating social risk.

Moreover, an expanding body of research suggests that NPI can play a health-promoting role in delaying the effect of a pandemic by reducing the overall and peak attack rate, and reducing cumulative mortality. Such measures could potentially provide valuable time for production and distribution of pandemic-strain vaccine and antiviral medication. Optimally, appropriate implementation of NPI also would decrease the burden on health care services and critical infrastructure. . . .

Some experts . . . refrain from recommending any course of action in the event of pandemic influenza. Yet such reticence runs contrary to the mission of public health and the common sense compulsion to act in the face of potential death or destruction.

The Challenges of Mandatory NPI

Broadly speaking, humans have organized mandatory NPI, such as quarantine and isolation, to mitigate the spread of contagion since antiquity. Until fairly recently, the needs, rights or even health of the afflicted (and quarantined) were rarely a primary concern among those administering such health orders. It was only in the years following the civil rights movements of the 1950s and 1960s that principles such as patient autonomy and the protection of civil liberties became legal and ethical cornerstones of public health programs aimed at mitigating infectious disease. It is important to remember the context in which mandatory NPI were implemented in 1918—an era characterized by medical paternalism and strong state authority to intervene with legal immunity in the lives of ordinary citizens.

Even so, the 1918 experience offers many examples of the application of mandatory NPI that backfired, potentially inciting undue social conflict that worsened disease transmission and, according to today's standards, would fall far short of ethical standards. In many cities, including San Francisco and Denver, local officials passed mask ordinances requiring individuals to wear layered-gauze masks in public, despite having no clear scientific proof of benefit, and authorizing the police to fine or arrest those who did not comply. These mandatory face mask laws proved to be bad policy. Many people wore the masks incorrectly, and some engaged in subterfuge to avoid wearing them. For others, the masks provided a false sense of security from the pandemic. There were even several instances where those who issued the mask order—including both San Francisco's mayor and health commissioner—were seen at public events with the masks dangling across their necks and not properly fastened. Some citizens formed antimask leagues and placarded the streets with antimask manifestos. There also was pushback to mandatory school closures and social distancing measures in many American cities during the fall of 1918, especially when these NPI were deactivated only to be reactivated days or weeks later when citizens felt that daily life was returning to some semblance of normality. In the worst instances, mandatory NPI pushback put society at greater risk of infection, and the haphazard application of NPI eroded the public trust. . . .

Setting Ethical Pandemic Policy

Mandatory NPI can be implemented in an ethical and efficacious manner if we hold certain ethical principles as ideals, with the strong caveat that mandatory NPI should only be considered in the event of a category 4 or 5 pandemic.

- To begin, mandatory NPI must rest on a foundation of public health science, coordination, and cooperation, not law enforcement.

- Second, NPI such as quarantine or school closures must meet the harm principle and conform to international ethical principles which require that "coercive public health measures be legitimate, legal, necessary, non-discriminatory and represent the least restrictive means appropriate to the reasonable achievement of public health goals."

- Finally, the principles of reciprocity, transparency, non-discrimination, and accountability—as well the right to due process to challenge mandatory NPI—must be enforced.

Mandatory NPI can be implemented in an ethical and efficacious manner if we hold certain ethical principles as ideals.

One of the greatest challenges for policymakers is to accurately determine during a pandemic unfolding in real time whether NPI meet the principle of proportionality—that the restrictions on individual liberties incurred by the NPI do not exceed what is needed to respond to a community's assessed risk. One of the most important lessons from previous epidemics is that it is easier to include ethical guidelines in a policy paper or a set of public health guidelines than it is to ensure they are met during a moment of crisis. Transparent application of NPI, with accountability and protection of civil liberties, is much more likely if communities have robust public health systems in place before a pandemic strikes. Indeed, the 1918 experience suggests that public health departments with longer track records of community involvement and compliance, and with clear delegation of roles and responsibilities, fared better. These issues, related to agency flow charts and community buy-in, are more pressing than ever given the various layers of public health that would be involved in any response to a category 4 or 5 pandemic in the United States and around the world. Excellent organization at the local level can be stymied if there is friction with county, state, or federal entities, not to mention private, international, or commercial actors.

Federal lawmakers and policymakers have a crucial role to play in establishing the framework in which individuals and communities can act in an empowered fashion to protect themselves during a pandemic. It is important to insist on a clear delineation of what federal laws and agencies will do and what local communities will do, and where they will obtain the resources. This will enable local communities to place voluntariness at the core of their NPI menu and clearly articulate when and how mandatory NPI would be employed. It has been abundantly clear over the past several years—as public and private organizations have focused on preparedness for any catastrophic event—that a diverse set of stakeholders must be included in any serious pandemic preparedness planning.

4

Pandemic Preparedness Planning Requires a Global Response

Harvey Rubin and C. Kameswara Rao

Harvey Rubin is the director of the University of Pennsylvania Institute for Strategic Threat Analysis and Response (ISTAR) and a member of the steering group of the Organization for Economic Cooperation and Development's Future Global Shocks project. C. Kameswara Rao is the executive secretary of the Foundation for Biotechnology Awareness and Education in Bangalore, India.

Infectious diseases and pandemics can have staggering social and economic impacts. Mitigating these impacts and addressing the challenges associated with infectious diseases requires a global response, such as a treaty, a compact, or an international convention. The establishment of an International Compact for Infectious Diseases would have four key missions: establishing a shared international data and knowledge base; establishing a network of international research centers; expanding the production of vaccines and therapeutics; and establishing international standards for best laboratory practices. The compact would help the world deal with pandemics and would benefit governments, the private sector, and academia, as well as people in developing and developed nations.

Harvey Rubin and C. Kameswara Rao, "An Enforceable International Compact for Infectious Diseases: Strategies to Operationalize New Initiatives to Strengthen Global Health Security," *Current Science*, vol. 96, no. 5, March 10, 2009. Reproduced by permission.

The predominance of infectious diseases has an undeniable moral significance and highlights our collective failure to give this problem, with implications for the economic well-being of both the developed and developing world, the attention it deserves. It is well recognized that infectious diseases perpetuate poverty in the developing world. They destroy family structure, and limit economic and educational opportunities affecting the economic security of all nations. While the social disintegration that follows an epidemic has filtered into the public consciousness, the consequent economic disruption is less known. A few weeks after the identification of the Severe Acute Respiratory Syndrome (SARS), the disease had already cost nearly US$ 30 billion, an amount sufficient to prevent 8 million deaths from infectious disease worldwide. A potential H5N1 [bird flu] pandemic costs much more, with economic losses approaching 600 billion dollars in the US alone, depending on the virulence of the strain. The spread of pathogenic bacteria that are becoming increasingly resistant to the existing antibiotics imposes a persistent cost in terms of both health and dollars.

Pandemic Threat Requires Global Effort

This formidable challenge calls for new strategies that integrate basic sciences, technology, and social, political, legal and economic realities. The solution should optimize trade-offs in the interplay of (a) international security, (b) global health, (c) creation and open dissemination of new knowledge and (d) maintenance and enhancement of the positive role of modern science on the economy of the developing world.

Over the past 25 years, there have been several successful efforts at resolving complex and sometimes overlooked international issues from the perspectives of both implementation and end-stage achievements.

Six NGOs [nongovernmental organizations] who met in October 1992 in New York founded the International Campaign to Ban Landmines (ICBL). Five years later, the International 'Convention on the Prohibition of the Use, Stockpiling, Production and Transfer or Anti-Personnel Mines and on Their Destruction' entered into force and the ICBL was awarded the Nobel Peace Prize 'as a model for similar processes in the future'. The essential issues surrounding infectious diseases possess similar normative force, which hopefully indicates a similar potential for progress.

The magnitude of the threat of infectious diseases also necessitates a major global, investigative effort.

The efforts of the Consultative Group on International Agricultural Research (CGIAR), under the leadership of the Nobel laureate Norman Borlaug, resulted in a massive increase in cereal yield in the second half of the 20th century, averting a global food crisis. CGIAR is an important antecedent combining North/South [Hemisphere] representation with innovative research and a truly lasting impact in some of the poorest regions in the world.

The magnitude of the threat of infectious diseases also necessitates a major global, investigative effort. The lasting positive impacts of international research centres are many, including fostering long-term relationships between scientists, establishing a culture of research responsibility and serving as the nucleus for safe applications of interdisciplinary sciences globally.

The key to any progress against infectious diseases is a structure that brings together diverse interests in a lasting manner. Without such a structure, the commitment to reducing the impact of infectious diseases on our national, economic and personal security will be subject to the political vagaries of the moment, leaving us unprepared for any health crisis.

Treaties, Conventions, and Compacts

There is no comprehensive programme for infectious diseases and the Biological and Toxin Weapons Convention is inadequate.

International treaties and conventions have some advantages like providing for an international legal basis for enforcement, creating a body of durable 'hard law' around an issue and drawing on the power of governments to regulate and license within their jurisdiction, but suffer from drawbacks such as ratification, will be slow and may limit action on urgent issues and the States may perceive enforcement clauses as an unacceptable burden, or even as a threat to their sovereignty.

While compacts have the benefits of being effective governance structures that are quick to set up and provide a framework for action, bring together a broad coalition of partners around a central issue and promote voluntary compliance of laboratories, companies, etc., the disadvantage is that enforcement relies on soft power and voluntary compliance, which may prove ineffective during a crisis.

The answer is a 'Comprehensive International Compact for Infectious Diseases', a two-pronged approach with the States as the eligible parties, and ratification as the method of participation. Treaty and compact are complementary systems that provide for parallel frameworks for different parties; the overall project will, over time, achieve the benefits of each. Domestic partners who are signatories to the compact can pressure States to comply with the treaty, as non-participation could put an organization/country at a disadvantage.

Several compact-like international agreements exist in such areas as human rights, environment, arms control and disarmament, and trade and finance.

Legitimacy and understanding of the overall system will be promoted through involvement of both the State and non-State actors.

International Compact for Infectious Diseases

Considering the general threat scenario of natural and deliberate spread of infectious diseases and the international consensus on preparing to face the threats, one of the authors (H.R. [Harvey Rubin]) with intellectual inputs from over a score of active microbiologists and pathologists, mostly from North America and Europe, has developed the 'International Compact for Infectious Diseases', with a four-point strategy for handling threats from infectious diseases:

Compact core mission I: Establish, maintain and monitor a shared international data and knowledge base for infectious diseases, including but not limited to biosurveillance information, relevant pharmaceutical data and suites of services and skills.

Compact core mission II: Establish, maintain and monitor a network of international basic sciences research centers that will support fundamental investigations into the pathophysiology of certain microbial threats to global health.

Compact core mission III: Expand capabilities for the production of vaccines and therapeutics expressly for emerging and reemerging infections.

Compact core mission IV: Establish, maintain and monitor international standards for best laboratory and regulatory practices.

Implementation of the four core missions of the compact will minimize the impact of infectious diseases on global health, social and economic development, and international security. The compact drives innovation and progress in four core areas: (a) information and knowledge sharing, (b) basic sciences, (c) drug and vaccine development and (d) best laboratory and regulatory practices. These missions are interconnected. Without a strong foundation of basic sciences, the drug and vaccine pipelines dry up. Similarly, in the absence of effective biosurveillance, it becomes difficult to project which strain of an emerging disease represents the most significant threat; which in turn hampers our ability to create counter-measures. Information technology [IT] and knowledge sharing will drive new science, which in turn can modify and inform regulatory initiatives. Standardized regulatory regimes enable new drugs and vaccines that will change global epidemiological patterns and these patterns must be reintegrated into a central database, beginning the cycle again.

Implementation of the four core missions of the compact will minimize the impact of infectious disease on global health, social and economic development, and international security.

There already exist a large number of databases that address one or more of the issues related to global health threats, for example, WHO's revised 2005 International Health Regulations. The information technology architecture proposed for the infectious disease compact will seamlessly integrate most of the existing databases, make them user-friendly yet provide the necessary security and add new data as recommended by the wide user community. Though the challenges here are formidable, they are hardly insurmountable. The greatest obstacle is the need for trust between signatory nations and a willingness to share data. There are technical challenges as well. Any attempt to create a common architecture for information systems would require common ontologies. New algorithms and models of disease spread need to be developed and validated. Lastly, the language of the compact has to address the issue of member States which do not report, or significantly under-report, the incidence of communicable diseases.

Biosurveillance and Reporting

International biosurveillance and reporting faces certain challenges, particularly at the level of sophistication envisioned, which include:

(a) Integrating current initiatives into a national health IT strategy and federal architecture to reduce the risk of duplicative efforts.

(b) Developing and adopting consistent interoperability standards.

(c) Creating an open architecture that maximizes the use of off-the-shelf tools.

(d) Creating enough flexibility to bring together disparate underlying IT languages and technologies to provide a common operating picture.

(e) Generating the ability to accept multiple data formats used by agencies that provide biosurveillance information.

(f) Generating the ability to feed information back to the originating agencies providing biosurveillance information in a format each agency can accept.

(g) Identifying data flows that will evolve during the developmental process.

(h) Allowing the methods of analysis to evolve and adapt as new data become available or existing datasets are improved.

(i) Knowing and evaluating the effectiveness of the current underlying algorithms, methods and structures for biosurveillance data analysis.

In order to accommodate the various interested parties and work within the limits of international law, the compact will embrace a two-pronged approach, working with States in the form of a treaty and with other interested parties (NGOs, academic institutions and the private sector) as a softer, pledge-based agreement.

By providing parallel frameworks for different parties, the overall project will achieve the benefits of each. Domestic groups that pledge their membership can apply pressure to their home States, hopefully speeding ratification of the treaty framework. By bringing together both State and non-State actors, the overall aims of the compact will be debated from a variety of different viewpoints, thereby enhancing the legitimacy of the project and promoting a thorough understanding of its goals.

The compact offers diverse stakeholder and community benefits, for which it is urgent to make accelerated efforts to draft, debate, refine, and implement the first ever International Compact for Infectious Diseases.

Anticipated Benefits

The compact offers diverse stakeholder and community benefits, for which it is urgent to make accelerated efforts to draft, debate, refine and implement the first ever International Compact for Infectious Diseases.

Addressing the problem as a whole creates powerful incentives for stakeholders to participate. For example, in order to access a central database containing information on current clinical trials, epidemiological data and new compounds and targets, participants would pledge to implement best laboratory and regulatory practices. By bringing together the government, private sector and academia, the compact allows each group to institutionalize their relations with the others. Pharmaceutical companies and public-private development partnerships can find partners to help take promising leads through to development. With the inclusion of post-marketing/post-distribution clinical trial data in the database, philanthropic organizations and governments will be able to understand the effects their investments will have throughout the world. Academics will acquire additional funding streams for their research as well as input from their colleagues all over the world. Finally, all parties will work together to harmonize regulatory processes across the board, reducing barriers to market entry for the much needed therapeutics and ensuring their wider distribution.

The compact is expected to afford the following benefits to communities from signatory nations in both the developed and developing worlds.

(a) Provide access to cheaper, more highly standardized specific therapeutics and vaccines that are relevant to the signatories.

(b) Ensure better quality control of vaccines, therapeutics and diagnostics in the developing world, leading to fewer expired or counterfeit agents.

(c) Provide access to and participation in high-level research.

(d) Provide developing and developed States with a voice in the direction of research and development.

(e) Distribute the costs and risks of research and development across a number of countries.

(f) Provide more complete datasets on emerging infections and potential pandemics.

(g) Create a more competitive market for vaccine and therapeutic development targeting diseases of relevance to signatory nations.

(h) Enhance and enable human health and well-being, economic development and basic biological research.

5

An International Pandemic Response Is an Excuse to Globalize the Planet

Jon Rappoport

Jon Rappoport is an American investigative journalist, author, and vice president of the publishing house Truth Seeker Company, Inc. He has written articles for CBS Healthwatch, Spin, Stern, Village Voice, *and* LA Weekly. *His books include* AIDS Inc.: Scandal of the Century, The Secret Behind Secret Societies, *and* Oklahoma Bombing: The Suppressed Truth.

Organizations such as the Council on Foreign Relations and the World Health Organization are using the public's fear of pandemics to justify the creation of an international medical bureaucracy. Many people who desire such a global organization attended an October 2009 symposium at which speakers repeated the false contention that pandemics created by novel diseases, such as the swine flu or the bird flu, pose a dire threat to the world. This fear mongering is a key part of the strategy to justify an international medical authority. People who are afraid will more easily accept the suggestion that the only way to respond to a pandemic is with a global response where individual nations surrender their national sovereignty.

The Council on Foreign Relations (CFR), headquartered in New York, is one of the key power centres pushing Globalism for All. As I've been writing for some time, medical

Jon Rappoport, "Swine Flu & Fake Epidemics: Medicalisation and the Push for Global Management," *New Dawn*, vol. 118, January/February, 2010. Copyright © New Dawn Magazine and Jon Rappoport. Reproduced by permission.

programs are a clever and deceptive strategy for advancing this goal—the coagulation of Earth under one system of political management.

Global control is not a "right-wing" fantasy. It's an objective much like the European Union, only writ much larger. Gradually, through attrition, sovereign nations decay under a super-bureaucracy that makes all the rules, issues the currency, and, over time, runs a tighter and tighter ship.

The outer shell of the CFR, founded 90 years ago as a Rockefeller plantation of control, is made up mostly of pundits and funded fellows and business leaders and politicians who look and sound like pompous blowhards. Which they are. But behind this mask, the inner CFR core designs schemes that could draw us all under the umbrella of de facto international control.

On October 16, 2009, the CFR held a symposium titled: *Pandemic Influenza: Science, Economics, and Foreign Policy.*

Much of the information in this symposium report is window dressing. However, it's worth noting a few comments made by presenters:

"*Laurie Garrett,* senior fellow for global health at the Council on Foreign Relations, said at the October 16, 2009 New York symposium that amid the array of unknowns surrounding the H1N1 virus, one certainty is that 'this is a worldwide event and it is occurring in the dawn of our age of globalisation.' Garrett added, 'It's a damn good thing we are dealing with a relatively mild flu this time, because clearly we are ill-prepared at this moment for a more virulent or more dangerous virus, either if this one takes on a more dangerous form ... or if a second totally different virus does emerge.' Helen Branswell of the Toronto-based *Canadian Press* agreed: 'We thought we were preparing for a more serious (bird flu H5N1) issue, but we are in fact not prepared for a mild one.'"

So two points were established early on: the Swine Flu is a mild disease, not a pandemic by any sensible definition; and leaders of "our age of globalisation" must be prepared for a more drastic disease event by taking worldwide measures now.

This latter issue is highlighted by another contributing CFR speaker:

"It was the overarching consensus of the symposium, first forwarded in the gathering by *Financial Times* correspondent *Andrew Jack* of London, that the current pandemic must serve as 'a teachable moment', focusing expert attention on the inherent contradictions in global governance of health issues, inequities in world access to vaccines and medical supplies, weaknesses in planning and management of epidemics with worldwide risks for economics and politics, and the public's respect for science and public health."

Andrew Jack thus punches up the notion that solutions to so-called global health problems can only be attained through international means.

Medical Crises and Global Governance

The report continues: "[Robert] Rubin [former US secretary of the Treasury and co-chair of the CFR] noted that the increased global interdependency of the current economy has changed the game for pandemic responses in the United States, leaving only one option: 'If the United States, and the world global economy, is going to be moderately well-prepared for this, there has to be an enormous amount of planning and agreed-upon processes and regimen decisions *before* the [pandemic] hits.'"

These speakers are talking about a *vast* system, a medical bureaucracy that can oversee planning and execution of "epidemic control" on a global scale.

Laurie Garrett then makes a pitch for equitable redistribution of wealth among nations:

"Moderator Garrett said: 'We have globalised [epidemic] risk and threat today, but not globalised benefits. So the whole world shares the risk of pandemic influenza, but only a small percentage share vaccines, medicines and treatments.'"

Who would make those wealth-redistributing decisions from the top? Who would allocate money and drugs and vaccines and doctors from Greenland to Tierra Del Fuego? There is only one answer: an internationally organised body that could override the wishes of sovereign countries.

Then John Lange sounds a sour note of failure in this regard:

"In face of profound scientific and economic insecurities, important foreign policy decisions must be made by the United States to address the globalisation of pandemic *protection* and benefits, as well as threat. Ambassador John E. Lange, of the Bill and Melinda Gates Foundation and former Special Representative on Avian and Pandemic Influenza for the State Department, said international coordination in response to the H5N1 pandemic [another mild flu season] of the 1990s paved the way for today's response to H1N1. Nevertheless, Lange said, little has been done to move towards a more institutionalised global response, due as much to a lack of political will as to strained resources, in spite of high expectations."

These [people] are talking about a vast system, a medical bureaucracy that can oversee planning and execution of "epidemic control" on a global scale.

Lange thus draws the problem. The US has lagged behind. The US is not eager enough for "a more institutionalised global response." The US doesn't want to cede power to some agency like the World Health Organisation (WHO).

Another speaker takes off the mask and drives home Lange's point harder:

"*Canadian Press*' Branswell doubted how feasible it will be for countries such as the United States and Canada to deliver on these expectations. At the heart of the debate is the issue of sovereignty, which may prevent states from carrying through with their agreements in the face of pandemic pressure, instead choosing to nationalise local supplies of vaccines, masks, protective gear and other medical supplies. Conversely, sovereignty has been invoked as the basis for refusing to share samples of dangerous flu viruses with WHO and international scientists, and for declining outside inspections of local outbreaks."

Surrendering National Sovereignty

Well, there it is. It doesn't take a genius to read between the lines. The surrender of national sovereignty is necessary if the world is going to deal with encroaching waves of pandemics. Nations will have to give up their independent status in these situations—and you can be sure that the international body formed to govern epidemic disease will be permanent. No one is stupid enough to think that the enormous effort and time and money needed to establish such a bureaucracy would fade away after the latest and greatest pandemic. Control would transfer now and in the future.

Medical crises, in this way, translate into further steps along the way to global governance.

No one is stupid enough to think that the enormous effort and time and money needed to establish such a bureaucracy would fade away after the latest and greatest pandemic.

Before citing more statements from the CFR symposium, let me offer some numbers on these "waves of world illness" we have endured over the last 15 years or so. *Keep in mind that epidemics are the primary justification for internationalisation of a medical monarchy.*

Total cases and deaths:

SARS [Severe Acute Respiratory Syndrome]—8,096 cases—774 deaths.

WEST NILE [VIRUS]—27,836 cases—1,088 deaths.

BIRD FLU—262 deaths.

SWINE FLU—On April 26, 2009, with 20 cases of Swine Flu in the US and no deaths, the US Dept. of Health and Human Services declared a nationwide public health emergency.

The WHO changed its definition of pandemic so that "enormous numbers of deaths and illness" was removed from the definition. This happened in May 2009.

Thus far, WHO estimates about 8,200 deaths from Swine Flu, worldwide. That would average out to about 15,000 deaths for the year. But the CDC [Centers for Disease Control and Prevention] claims 36,000 people die every year from *ordinary flu* in the US alone.

So far, the global count of Swine Flu cases is 587,653.

Yet WHO states, "Every winter, tens of millions of people get the [ordinary] flu. Most are only ill and out of work for a week, yet the elderly are at a higher risk of death from the illness. We know the worldwide death toll exceeds a few hundred thousand people a year . . ."

Fear Mongering

So why is Swine Flu a pandemic, and why is ordinary flu not a pandemic?

Fear mongering is about NEW diseases. That's why.

It gets worse.

In early November [2009], an explosive report by Sharyl Attkisson hit the CBS News website: Of all the probable or suspected swine flu cases in California actually tested by state labs since July 2009, based on 13,704 tests, only 2% of the patients had Swine Flu. 12% had some other kind of flu. And a whopping 86% didn't have flu at all.

In Florida, based on 8,853 tests for suspected/probable Swine Flu, only 17% had Swine Flu. 83% were negative for other flu. So 83% didn't have ANY kind of flu.

In Alaska, based on 722 tests for suspected/probable Swine Flu, only 11% had Swine Flu. In Georgia, based on 3,117 tests, only 2% had Swine Flu.

When the CFR is talking about globalizing pandemic responses, and nations surrendering their sovereignty, it's all based on an epidemic cover story that is patently false.

My point here is this: All these recent "epidemics" have been outright fakes. The numbers of cases and deaths are miniscule compared with older traditional illnesses—for which no pandemic emergencies have been declared.

Therefore, when the CFR is talking about globalising pandemic responses, and nations surrendering their sovereignty, it's all based on an epidemic cover story that is patently false. It's like saying, "The sky is falling. You have to lend all your support to the construction of a dome that will shield us from the lethal debris. A global 'health czar' will be in charge of building and maintaining the dome, and all governments must bow to his orders, which are given to protect everyone."

Continuing now with the CFR symposium report: We come to the toxic portion of the issue. In many nations, there has been vigorous debate over the use of so-called adjuvants in flu vaccines. One such substance, squalene, has been banned in several countries, because it can have dangerous effects. But the CFR would apparently like to override this question and promote universal use of squalene in vaccines, despite the glaring fact that Swine Flu itself is so mild the risks of the vaccine far outweigh its need.

"While recently the [Barack] Obama administration brokered a deal among eleven wealthy nations to donate 10 percent of their vaccine supply of H1N1 to WHO for use in developing countries, Canada has not signed on, in an uncharacteristic decision. . . . On the other hand, the Obama administration has refused the use of adjuvants, which are used in Europe, Canada and Japan to stretch out the antigen supply for wider global use, causing Lange to question the role of the United States as a true 'global player'. Adjuvants help trigger the immune response, allowing dilution of precious flu antigens so that upwards of ten times as many people can be immunised with the same antigen supply. If the US were using adjuvant in its H1N1 vaccines, the country could be in a position to offer sufficient surplus product to WHO to bring the agency's supply for poor countries up by hundreds of millions of doses."

Not "a true global player." That epithet carries considerable weight in CFR and allied circles. It means, "Let's watch this person. If he wants our support, he's going to have to change his tune. Let him understand that."

Combating Anti-Vaccine Hype

Finally, the CFR report takes a swipe at people who are educating themselves on the historical toxicity of vaccines. And here, it does:

"The public perception of swine flu has further complicated the issue, causing both public doubt and panic at the same time. Branswell fears that 'the WHO has lost control of the message', allowing misinformed threats, such as the current anti-vaccine hype, to resonate around the world as the scientific community races to catch up with the facts.

"The last great flu pandemic of 1968 occurred in a deeply divided world, where entire regions of the planet were no-travel zones for billions of people. It was an era of telephones and posted mail, evening newscasts, and morning newspapers. Both viruses and information spread comparatively slowly.

"Though today the vaccine methods of production and distribution mirror those practiced a half-century ago, the age of globalisation has ushered in rapid human and animal travel, leading to worldwide spread of viruses. The internet has similarly opened the door to viral spread of disease truths, half-truths and outright lies. Thankfully, the mild H1N1 has offered the world community an opportunity to see these 21st Century challenges without simultaneously experiencing worst-case outcomes. It is a teachable moment, but it remains to be seen whether—on both global and local scales—governments, companies and individuals are learning."

What better way to reframe this incriminating picture than to claim that a few politically neutral germs are the agents of death.

Twenty years ago, when I was writing my first book, *AIDS INC.*, I realised that medical propaganda could be used as a pre-eminent tool in controlling populations, because doctors and public health bureaucrats exude an air of political neutrality.

These esteemed figures appear to have no agenda of a political or economic nature. They speak as minor saints. They always "care and share." When they say citizens must take certain actions to protect themselves and their loved ones, they speak with great authority.

Under that flag, much destruction can be wrought. For example, in certain areas of Africa, people have been dying from the same causes for hundreds of years: protein-calorie malnutrition; outright starvation; gross lack of sanitation; overcrowding; contaminated water supplies; abject poverty; no hope; and more recently, vaccines and medical drugs which, administered to people whose immune systems are already devastatingly compromised, can be lethal.

At the root of these causes is stolen land. Colonisation by governments and then mega-corporations, and brutal repression by local dictators—such controllers want to conceal their own naked actions, and they also want to keep hidden the actual immediate causes of death in Africa—the causes they, the controllers, invoke and maintain.

What better way to reframe this incriminating picture than to claim that a few politically neutral germs are the agents of death. Then, you can build a few showplace hospitals, bring in a bevy of doctors, set up a lab or two and demand that pharmaceutical companies donate medicines for the suffering. Meanwhile, no one cleans up the water, no one restores good land to the dispossessed, and no one alleviates the massively overcrowded living conditions.

Isolate any germ under the sun, give any medicine, as long as the fundamental horrendous facts of life remain the same, people will die in great numbers, and those in control will remain in control.

Globalizing "Humanitarian Solutions"

The CFR is part of a sophisticated operation to globalise "humanitarian solutions" under the rubric of medical care. Its main ally is the World Health Organisation, an agency of the UN [United Nations]. Near the close of World War II, members of the CFR were, in fact, tapped to write the basic outline of the soon-to-be created UN.

The WHO is on the march. It is trying to insert itself and its rulings and demands into the governments of many nations. In 2003, it won its biggest one-shot victory. Through fraudulent travel advisories, based on non-science, it raised fears about SARS (at best, a tiny illness) and managed to effectively shut down air travel in and out of Toronto. Toronto lost several billion dollars in the process. I was a peripheral part of a budding effort to convince local business owners to file a lawsuit. At first, there was some enthusiasm, but then it faded out. The people of Toronto knuckled under, some of them lost their shirts, and they plowed on.

The WHO is, by far, the most successful agency of the UN. It has emerged as the rising star of that moribund organisation. It has delivered victories because it is flying under the banner of medical power. The modern priesthood.

CFR, its inner core, is well aware that medical control is a trump card it can play to great advantage. The October [2009] Symposium was an event with such an edge.

There is an ultimate vision here that at least a few major power players entertain: subsume every citizen of planet Earth under a network of authoritarian medical control—as part of a global-management political system.

This is no one time takeover by force. This is no crashing coup. In intelligence-agency parlance, it's a step-operation. A little progress here, a little progress there. Speakers at the Symposium called Swine Flu "a teaching moment." By this they meant two things. This mild flu gives CFR and its allies a chance to expand their global influence, through the expansion of public-health agencies, most notably WHO and the American CDC. And the population of the planet is "taught" to respect so-called epidemics and the resulting missives that come down from their leaders.

The pace of these fake epidemics and the accompanying media propaganda is quickening. There is an ultimate vision here that at least a few major power players entertain: subsume every citizen of planet Earth under a network of authoritarian medical control—as part of a global-management political system.

Cradle to grave, every person is diagnosed with at least several diseases or mental disorders and falls under the continuing treatment of doctors. These treatments are, for the most part, toxic. That is to say, they weaken the immune system and scramble neurotransmitter systems of the brain. People become less able to take effective action in *any* direction. People everywhere become fixated on their diseases. They become less able to maintain their freedom. They view themselves as lifelong patients.

In case you think this is pure fantasy, let me recite a few facts about the US medical-care system. These numbers are based in part, but not wholly, on a landmark paper published on July 26, 2000, in the *Journal of the American Medical Association*. The paper was titled, "Is US Health Really the Best in the World?" The author was Barbara Starfield, who was then associated with the Johns Hopkins School of Public Health. In other words, this was a mainstream piece of work all the way.

Each year in the US there are:

- 12,000 deaths from unnecessary surgeries;

- 7,000 deaths from medication error in hospitals;

- 20,000 deaths from other errors in hospitals;

- 80,000 deaths from infections acquired in hospitals;

- 106,000 deaths from FDA [Food and Drug Administration]-approved correctly prescribed medicines.

The total of medically-caused deaths in the US every year is 225,000.

This makes the medical system the third leading cause of death in the US, behind heart disease and cancer.

Then if you multiply these numbers by all the people who are emotionally involved in, and temporarily paralysed by, the deaths of these 225,000 Americans, you begin to see the fuller picture of the effects on every level. And all this is just in America.

In, say, Africa, the diversion of attention, by medical propaganda and cover stories, from the *real* causes of millions of annual deaths? How can one even begin to calculate those effects?

If, over the next 10 or 20 years, CFR and its allies, with direct intent or even blind do-good hope, make large strides toward globalising a medical bureaucracy that would oversee the "health of the planet," consider what that will do, what consequences that will have.

6

The World Must Ensure Equal Access to Pandemic Flu Vaccines

Tadataka Yamada

Tadataka "Tachi" Yamada is president of the global health program at the Bill & Melinda Gates Foundation. Before joining the foundation, he served as chairman of research and development at GlaxoSmithKline and was chairman of the Department of Internal Medicine at the University of Michigan Medical School.

Influenza pandemics pose a serious threat to the global community, particularly to those who live in the developing world. Fortunately, pharmaceutical companies are on track to develop an effective vaccine against the H1N1 (swine) influenza virus. When an effective vaccine is developed, it is morally imperative that everyone in the world, both rich and poor, have equal access to it. Vaccine manufacturing capacity, cost, and delivery infrastructure challenges must be overcome in order to ensure equal vaccine access. Rich countries, vaccine manufacturers, and regulatory agencies all have responsibilities to ensure that everyone in the world has access to life-saving vaccines.

On June 11, 2009, Margaret Chan, director general of the World Health Organization (WHO), declared that the status of the influenza A (H1N1) pandemic had reached phase

Tadataka Yamada, "Poverty, Wealth, and Access to Pandemic Influenza Vaccines," *New England Journal of Medicine*, vol. 361, no. 12, September 17, 2009. Copyright © 2009 Massachusetts Medical Society. Reproduced by permission of the Massachusetts Medical Society.

6—active transmission on a global scale. Until now, the case fatality rate of this influenza has been quite low, but history teaches us that the situation could take a turn for the worse during the next wave of the pandemic. If a 1918-like pandemic were to occur today, tens of millions of people could die, the vast majority of them in the world's poorest countries.

Fortunately, the prospects for developing an effective vaccine to prevent infection with the current H1N1 virus are excellent, and the world's pharmaceutical companies are working diligently at this task. In contemplating equal access to such a vaccine, it is important to consider three key issues: manufacturing capacity, cost, and delivery.

Only a few countries in the world have plants for manufacturing influenza vaccine, and three companies—GlaxoSmithKline, Sanofi-Aventis, and Novartis—account for most of the world's manufacturing capacity. The number of doses of vaccine against H1N1 influenza that could be produced with the existing capacity is very large, but the sobering truth is that even if production were switched over completely from seasonal influenza vaccine to pandemic influenza vaccine, there would not be nearly enough for everyone in the world. The size of the gap in potential supply depends greatly on the dose that is required, and it may be possible to reduce the necessary dose by as much as 75% with the use of an adjuvant. The challenging problem is that much, if not most, of the manufacturing capacity is already spoken for through purchasing contracts held by many of the world's wealthy countries.

The second issue is cost. Despite the enormous technological investment required to create a vaccine, the traditional cost of seasonal influenza vaccines even in wealthy countries is quite low. For the pandemic H1N1 influenza vaccine, the major manufacturers have indicated a willingness to offer tiered pricing, with affordable prices for poor countries. Going even further, Sanofi-Aventis has committed to donating 100 million doses of its vaccine to a stockpile for poor countries, and GlaxoSmithKline has committed to donating 50 million doses. Nevertheless, financial commitments from wealthy countries will be needed to help poorer countries purchase vaccines—cost should not be a barrier to access.

Rich countries have a responsibility to stand in line and receive their vaccine allotments alongside poor countries, even if they have paid for their vaccine before others could do so.

Finally, the scope of access to vaccines will in part be determined by the infrastructure required to deliver them to all citizens in mass campaigns. Ironically, poor countries may have an advantage on this front, since many have recent experience with mass campaigns involving vaccines against polio, measles, and hepatitis B; delivery may therefore be less of a challenge for them, provided that the vaccines reach them in a timely fashion. By contrast, in many wealthier countries, such campaigns have not been undertaken for some time. Getting the vaccine to large numbers of young adults, in particular, may be a formidable task for which preparations must surely be made as soon as possible.

Our limited capacity for producing potentially lifesaving vaccines presents a pressing moral challenge. I believe wholeheartedly that all lives have equal value (this is the basic principle motivating the Bill and Melinda Gates Foundation, where I work), and I believe that every stakeholder has a responsibility to ensure that the pandemic does not take a 1918-like toll on the world. We have therefore worked with partner stakeholders to develop a proposed set of principles to guide the global allocation of pandemic vaccine (see box [not included]).

Rich countries have a responsibility to stand in line and receive their vaccine allotments alongside poor countries, even if they have paid for their vaccine before others could do so. It would be inexcusable to force poor countries to wait until the rich have been served under their existing contracts with vaccine manufacturers. Moreover, rich countries must also consider how they can provide contributions to offset the cost of vaccines for countries that cannot afford to pay for them. Countries that are home to influenza-vaccine manufacturing plants have a special responsibility to avoid nationalizing those facilities in an effort to reserve their output for their own citizens before others. And all countries must prepare now for the rapid delivery of the vaccines as soon as they become available.

Manufacturers have a responsibility to apply their full capabilities to creating the greatest possible quantity of vaccine doses. Despite contractual obligations to supply many wealthy countries with their vaccines, manufacturers must resist the temptation to commit all their capacity to those who can pay the most. This is not a time to adhere to the "first come, first served" model of business, since we may be facing a health crisis of global proportions in which all people and countries are equally at risk. To ensure fairness, full adherence to a tiered pricing scheme in which the cost to the purchaser is proportionate to its ability to pay is essential. The generous donations made by Sanofi-Aventis and GlaxoSmithKline set an example that all manufacturers should emulate. In return for their responsible actions, it would be reasonable for manufacturers to be indemnified against liability from potential adverse reactions to their vaccines.

Regulatory agencies have an important responsibility in this impending crisis because they stand between the manufacturers of pandemic influenza vaccines and the people who will benefit from them. It is critically important that regulators apply their usual rigorous standards in approving the new vaccines—but also that they do so in a timely fashion. A special task facing them is the rapid review and consideration of the safety and efficacy of adjuvants, whose use could greatly reduce the required dose of vaccine and thereby expand the number of doses that could be manufactured.

The WHO has provided strong leadership as the world has contemplated the prospect of an influenza pandemic. We are counting on the organization to guide us, wisely and fairly, through the complex challenges that lie ahead.

Regulatory agencies have an important responsibility in this impending crisis because they stand between the manufacturers of pandemic influenza vaccines and the people who will benefit from them.

The prospect of a worsening global influenza pandemic is real and will not go away anytime soon. I cannot imagine standing by and watching if, at the time of crisis, the rich live and the poor die. It will take collective commitment and action by all of us to prevent this from happening.

7

Negotiating Equal Access to Pandemic Flu Vaccines Will Be Difficult

David P. Fidler

David P. Fidler is a professor of law and the director of the Center on American and Global Security at Indiana University. He is a leading expert on international law, global health, and the biosecurity threats posed by biological weapons and bioterrorism.

Concerns about equal access to vaccines emerge each time an influenza virus threatens to cause a pandemic. Unfortunately, the response of developed countries during past pandemic threats reveals the difficulty in negotiating equal vaccine access. Developing countries want to require richer countries to share costly vaccines; however, richer countries want to rely on inconsistent and voluntary activities that preserve their national self-interests. Since no legal basis in international law currently exists to require the sharing of vaccines or drugs, negotiations are the only way forward. Negotiating an equitable distribution path for vaccines, however, represents a difficult challenge.

One of the most controversial areas of global health diplomacy over the past five years [2005–2010] has involved negotiations to increase equitable access to vaccines for highly pathogenic avian influenza A (H5N1) (HPAI-H5N1) and pandemic 2009 influenza A (H1N1) (2009-H1N1). The limited

David P. Fidler, "Negotiating Equitable Access to Influenza Vaccines: Global Health Diplomacy and the Controversies Surrounding Avian Influenza H5N1 and Pandemic Influenza H1N1," *PLoS Medicine*, vol. 7, no. 5, May 2010. Copyright © 2010 David P. Fidler. Reproduced by permission.

results produced by these negotiations have stimulated calls for a new global framework to improve equitable access to influenza vaccines. The prospects for such a framework are not, however, promising, because the national interests of most developed states vis-à-vis dangerous influenza strains favor retaining the existing imbalanced, reactive, and ad hoc approach to vaccine access. This article examines why negotiating equitable access to influenza vaccines in the context of HPAI-H5N1 and 2009-H1N1 has been, and promises to continue to be, a difficult diplomatic endeavor.

Vaccine Access Controversies

The re-emergence of HPAI-H5N1 in 2004 and its spread triggered fears that the world was on the brink of a potentially devastating influenza pandemic. Preparations for pandemic influenza frantically began, and included plans to develop a vaccine for a pandemic H5N1 strain. These plans ran headlong into developing-country concerns that their populations would not have access to H5N1 vaccines. These concerns, and the lack of any mechanism to ensure equitable access to vaccines and other benefits from research on influenza viruses, prompted Indonesia, in 2007, to refuse to share H5N1 virus samples with the World Health Organization (WHO) that would be used for surveillance. Supported by many developing countries, Indonesia's action questioned the legitimacy of WHO's Global Influenza Surveillance Network and forced WHO and its member states to begin negotiations to create a new system of influenza virus and benefits sharing. Although WHO member states agreed to establish a stockpile of H5N1 vaccine, the negotiations have, to date, failed to reach agreement.

Concerns about equitable access flared again in 2009 when a novel strain of influenza A (H1N1) emerged and spread around the world. The speed and ease with which the 2009-H1N1 strain moved meant that a vaccine was the only practical means of preventing infection, and efforts to produce a vaccine began in the late spring and early summer. Developed countries placed large advance orders for 2009-H1N1 vaccine and bought virtually all the vaccine companies could manufacture. Developing countries and WHO identified the lack of equity in how developed countries were securing access to the vaccine. WHO entered talks with manufacturers and developed-country governments to secure some vaccine for developing countries, and WHO and the United Nations (UN) appealed for monetary donations to purchase vaccines and other supplies to help developing countries address the 2009-H1N1 virus. These efforts yielded donation pledges from manufacturers and developed countries, but the donations still left the developing world with limited supplies compared to developed countries, which would retain, even after donations, sufficient vaccine to cover their populations.

Feared and actual problems with 2009-H1N1 vaccine production, however, affected the amount and timing of vaccine available for developing countries. As of this writing [May 4, 2010,] Canada had not joined other developed-countries in pledging to donate vaccines, because of shortages within Canada, and Canada awarded its vaccine contract to a Canadian company because it feared that foreign governments might restrict exports to Canada because of vaccine shortages within their territories. The Australian government made it clear to the Australian manufacturer CSL that it must fulfill the government's domestic needs before exporting vaccine to the United States. The United States pledged on September 17, 2009, to donate 10% of its vaccine purchases to WHO, but on October 28, US Secretary of Health and Human Services Kathleen Sebelius stated that the United States would not donate H1N1 vaccine as promised until all at-risk Americans had access, because production problems had created shortages in the United States. These fears and actions reinforced the sense that the status quo concerning equitable access to influenza vaccines for developing countries was flawed.

Call for a Global Access Framework

The unsatisfactory nature of vaccine access concerning HPAI-H5N1 and 2009-H1N1 has created interest in creation of a global framework for equitable access that would become operational *before* the next influenza crisis. In a presentation to the Forum of Microbial Threats of the Institute of Medicine in September 2009, WHO's lead influenza specialist, Keiji Fukuda, described the problems experienced with the negotiations on HPAI-H5N1 virus and benefits sharing and on obtaining donations from manufacturers and developed countries for 2009-H1N1 vaccine. Fukuda emphasized that the process and outcomes of the negotiations were suboptimal in terms of both public health and global equity and justice. Other experts have made similar claims concerning the moral and social justice issues at stake in equitable access to 2009-H1N1 vaccines. In the interests of global health and global solidarity, Fukuda argued that a framework was needed to support global responses to influenza threats and ensure equitable access to vaccines for developing countries. He asserted that improving access is the central global governance issue of our times, which gives the need for a global access framework importance beyond the world of public health.

Negotiating Equitable Access

Negotiations to increase access to vaccines for HPAI-H5N1 and 2009-H1N1 have not proved successful for many reasons. In the Intergovernmental Meeting (IGM) on Pandemic Influenza Preparedness Framework for the Sharing of Influenza Viruses and Access to Vaccines and Other Benefits, WHO member states failed to reach agreement because they could not agree on benefit sharing. Developing countries want obligatory benefit sharing in return for virus sharing, with binding terms spelled out in a Standard Material Transfer Agreement (SMTA). In contrast, developed countries want to avoid binding obligations to provide benefits (e.g., vaccines, antivirals) in exchange for access to virus samples provided by developing countries. At least one news report indicated that developed countries wanted to avoid losing their ability to place advance orders for influenza vaccine because of a binding SMTA.

Interestingly, the 2009-H1N1 outbreak was under way when the IGM negotiations concluded unsuccessfully, meaning that this latest influenza threat was not a "game changer" for the positions staked out by WHO member states. In fact, the manner in which the outbreak and vaccine development and use proceeded favored developed countries for two reasons. First, countries with cases of 2009-H1N1 shared virus samples with WHO for surveillance and vaccine development without a *quid pro quo* for benefit sharing. To date, Indonesia remains the only country that has refused to share virus samples; other developing countries, even those that have supported Indonesia, share their samples without requiring benefits in return. Second, developed countries were able, through advance purchase contracts, to access almost all the vaccine existing manufacturing facilities can produce in order to ensure they would have 2009-H1N1 vaccine for their populations—precisely the option developed countries do not want the proposed SMTA to affect.

Negotiations to increase access to vaccines for HPAI-H5N1 and 2009-H1N1 have not proved successful for many reasons.

In terms of vaccine for 2009-H1N1, donations from manufacturers and developed countries were not the product of real negotiations, given that WHO and developing countries had little leverage to influence developed countries other than rhetoric about equity, justice, and solidarity. As experts noted, the donations from manufacturers were initially made without a fixed delivery date, meaning that the donated vaccines might arrive too late to be of much benefit in developing countries.

Developed countries only agreed to make donations *after* (1) they learned, unexpectedly, that a one-dose regimen would immunize adults, which doubled the amount of vaccine available; and (2) data from the Northern and Southern hemispheres revealed that the 2009-H1N1 virus was behaving as a mild virus and not as a killer strain, which reduced the threat the virus posed. In addition, developed countries pledging donations made sure that they had enough vaccine to cover their populations or, as happened with the United States, postponed donations in order to address national needs. In essence, manufacturers and developed countries incurred minimal financial, national public health, or political costs in pledging and, if necessary, delaying vaccine donations.

Access in International Law

What has transpired in the contexts of HPAI-H5N1 and 2009-H1N1 reflects patterns seen in other efforts to create equitable access for vaccines and drugs. Existing international legal regimes that support global health, such as the WHO Constitution, the "right to health" in human rights treaties, and the International Health Regulations 2005, do not contain specific, binding provisions on equitable access to vaccines and drugs for developing countries. WHO's interest in creating a new global framework rather than relying on existing legal agreements reinforces the lack of any specific equitable access regime. Efforts to generate equitable access are not operated through purpose-built international legal instruments, and these efforts include WHO's adoption of a nonbinding global strategy on public health, innovation, and intellectual property, provision of vaccines and drugs by intergovernmental organizations (e.g., WHO, UNICEF [UN Children's Fund]); bilateral donation schemes (e.g., the [US] President's Emergency Plan for AIDS Relief); and public-private and nongovernmental mechanisms that make vaccines and drugs more available to developing countries (e.g., the Global Fund to Fight AIDS,

Tuberculosis, and Malaria; the GAVI [Global Alliance for Vaccines and Immunisation] Alliance; [Bill] Clinton Global Initiative; Médecins Sans Frontières' [Doctors Without Borders'] Campaign for Access to Essential Medicines; the International Finance Facility for Immunization; UNITAID; and Advance Market Commitments for Vaccines).

This reality provides insight into why negotiations on virus and benefit sharing in connection with HPAI-H5N1 have, to date, failed, and why negotiations on a global access framework in the wake of the problems surrounding 2009-H1N1 would face obstacles. In short, states have not agreed to binding arrangements on more equitable access but, rather, attempt to increase such access through ad hoc, reactive, and nonbinding activities that preserve national freedom of action while demonstrating some humanitarian concern.

Moreover, the situation concerning access to vaccines and drugs reflects how states generally allocate control of and access to resources. The central principles for allocating resources in international law are (1) sovereignty for resources found within a state's territory, and (2) exclusive jurisdiction or control for resources found seawards from coastal states (e.g., the Exclusive Economic Zone in the law of the sea). International relations provide few, if any, examples of states' establishing a global framework to allocate resources, or the benefits derived from their exploitation, equitably. The most famous effort occurred in the negotiation of the UN Convention on the Law of the Sea (UNCLOS) in the 1970s and early 1980s and involved designating mineral resources found beyond 200 nautical miles from coastal states as the "common heritage of mankind," which would be exploited under jurisdiction of an International Seabed Authority, with benefits accruing to developing countries. However, the United States and other developed countries opposed this aspect of UNCLOS, which, because of this opposition, has been revised to reflect what these developed countries prefer concerning exploitation of these mineral resources.

The problems of equitable access to vaccines and drugs reflect these larger patterns in international law and international relations. As Indonesia's assertion of "viral sovereignty" demonstrates, states have sovereignty over biological samples isolated within their territories. Negotiations within the WHO and the IGM have re-emphasized that states have sovereignty over biological resources found within their jurisdictions. Similarly, states in which vaccines and drugs are manufactured have sovereignty over the manufacturing process and the products themselves, until they are exported. States that import vaccines and drugs then have sovereignty over such resources and, absent a binding obligation, may allocate them however they wish. Negotiations to create a global access framework that more equitably distributes influenza vaccines would need to navigate through triple claims of sovereignty—a very tall order, without even factoring in the divergence of national interests seen in the IGM negotiations on virus and benefit sharing and the access problems associated with vaccine for 2009-H1N1.

Negotiations on a global access framework in the wake of the problems surrounding 2009-H1N1 would face obstacles.

A Difficult Challenge

Increasing equitable access to vaccines for dangerous influenza strains represents a difficult challenge for global health diplomacy, a challenge this article has addressed in only a preliminary manner. Efforts to recalibrate virus- and benefit-sharing in connection with HPAI-H5N1 through intergovernmental negotiations have not, so far, been successful. The manner in which access to vaccine for 2009-H1N1 played out highlights why the interests of developed and developing countries diverge in this context, and the reasons behind this divergence deserve deeper study. Existing international legal regimes on global health provide no templates for negotiating the new global access framework that WHO and others perceive is necessary. Similarly, negotiations for equitable access to resources, or the benefits of their exploitation, have generally failed in other areas of international relations, dimming prospects that precedents for a global access framework for pandemic influenza vaccines can be found outside the global health context. The default rules for allocating resources in international law rely on the principle of sovereignty, and these rules hold in the context of virus samples and vaccine supplies, as demonstrated with HPAI-H5N1 and 2009-H1N1.

Increasing equitable access to vaccines for dangerous influenza strains represents a difficult challenge for global health diplomacy.

Even the emergence of the first pandemic strain of influenza in 40 years in 2009 did not break the pattern of state behavior with respect to equitable access to a valuable but scarce resource. The appearance of a more severe influenza strain will reinforce rather than overcome this pattern, because developed countries will prize their power and flexibility of action more in a severe pandemic than in a mild one, thus making hope for a crisis-sparked breakthrough misguided. The negotiating path that could lead to a new global access framework for influenza vaccines is not apparent, especially in a context in which aggregate global production capacity is woefully inadequate, the geographic location of production facilities is concentrated in developed countries, timelines for developing new vaccines create problems for rapid prevention strategies, and existing manufacturing technologies and distribution systems require improvements.

The need to increase global production capacity, diversify locales for manufacturing facilities, decrease the time from "lab to jab," and reduce production and distribution uncertainties, has been recognized for years without sufficient progress being made, as evidenced by the HPAI-H5N1 and 2009-H1N1 controversies. Further research is required on ways in which states and non-state actors can address these problems through negotiated collective action. The diplomatic environment may have been made more difficult by accusations made and hearings held by officials in the Council of Europe that WHO succumbed to pressure from the pharmaceutical industry to declare a "false pandemic" and support development and use of a vaccine. In the environment that exists on these issues, diplomatic advances will not be made simply by repeated claims that an undefined "global framework" is required because more equitable access is the just and moral end all states should seek.

8

A Universal Flu Vaccine Could Preempt a Pandemic

Kelly Morris

Kelly Morris writes for The Lancet Infectious Diseases *journal, a monthly journal of original research, review, opinion, and news covering international issues relevant to clinical infectious diseases.*

A universal flu vaccine could protect humans against pandemic flu viruses. Current pandemic preparedness depends on vaccines that are produced after a pandemic threat has been identified. This means that there always is a lag time between when a pandemic begins and when vaccine is available. This lag time could be deadly. If a universal vaccine were available, it could be manufactured and administered on a routine basis and preemptively protect against a pandemic. Research strategies to produce a universal vaccine have been promising and should be pursued.

A vaccine that provides broad immunity to many influenza strains—a pan-influenza or universal vaccine—could be used pre-emptively to protect against seasonal and pandemic influenza. Concern over the delay in vaccine availability during the 2009 H1N1 pandemic has increased the pressure to develop pre-emptive approaches. New findings from studies of the H1N1 pandemic and new vaccine approaches are now providing a better insight into what is needed for pre-emptive protection.

Kelly Morris, "Influenza Protection—Natural Immunity and New Vaccines," *The Lancet Infectious Diseases*, vol. 11, April 2011. Reproduced by permission of Elsevier Sciences.

The Virological Holy Grail

"A universal flu vaccine has been the Holy Grail for influenza virologists and vaccine manufacturers for a long time now", notes Heath Kelly, head of epidemiology at the Victorian Infectious Diseases Reference Laboratory (North Melbourne, Australia). The issue in Australia, as in many industrialised countries, was that an effective pandemic H1N1 vaccine was not available until the outbreak was past its peak. Kelly believes that "this pandemic has confirmed that current vaccine manufacturing technology, combined with accepted regulatory requirements, will always provide a vaccine intended to be available in significant quantity too late, at least in one hemisphere."

A universal flu vaccine has been the Holy Grail for influenza virologists and vaccine makers for a long time now.

If pandemic H1N1 had been more like the avian influenza strain H5N1, with even 5% mortality, the gap between the beginning of the pandemic and the availability of vaccine—at least 6–9 months—could have caused "mayhem", in terms of mortality and the stress on health systems and society, says Andrew McMichael, professor of molecular medicine at the Weatherall Institute of Molecular Medicine (Oxford University, UK). "Between now and the next pandemic there is some pressure to prevent that scenario." Improvements in drug treatments could offer some pandemic control, but are unlikely to be affordable in much of the world, "whereas an effective, safe vaccine could be made more widely available", he says.

Vaccines designed annually against seasonal influenza strains are often well matched to circulating strains so they produce protective antibody responses. However, seasonal vaccines do not match well with emergent strains, making pandemic protection unpredictable. "It is still a far off goal but a universal vaccine, if it were possible, could provide once-in-a lifetime protection", says McMichael, offering both protection against future pandemics and 20–30 years of immunity against seasonal influenza. Uptake and roll-out would greatly improve, while alleviating production and distribution pressures, he suggests.

The first broadly protective vaccines might need to be manufactured and administered more regularly, although less than annually, but this would still allow routine manufacturing and administration, says Kelly. Together with an in-built surge capacity, "a truly universal effective vaccine may solve the problems with pandemic preparedness being highlighted over H1N1", Kelly told *TID* [*The Lancet Infectious Diseases*]. Recent findings suggest several potential approaches to develop such vaccines.

A universal vaccine, if it were possible, could provide once-in-a-lifetime protection.

Production Strategies

During the H1N1 pandemic, Patrick Wilson (University of Chicago, IL, USA) and his team isolated antibodies from patients with clinical disease, with the aim of producing antibodies to treat severely ill patients. In January, 2011, the team reported that the antibody response against the pandemic H1N1 strain's coat protein, haemagglutinin, was unexpectedly broad. "Unlike antibodies elicited by annual influenza vaccinations, most neutralising antibodies induced by pandemic H1N1 infection were broadly cross-reactive against epitopes [the parts of a molecule to which an antibody binds] in the haemagglutinin stalk and head domain of multiple influenza strains", explains Wilson and colleagues. Five of the isolated antibodies could bind all the seasonal H1N1 strains from the past decade, the devastating 1918 pandemic H1N1 strain—

estimated to have killed 50 million people between 1918 and 1920—and a potentially lethal H5N1 avian influenza strain.

The team speculate that these antibody responses developed through cross-reactivity to functionally important epitopes on haemagglutinin that are widely conserved between many viral strains. "This suggests that a pan-influenza vaccine may be possible, given the right immunogen", the researchers note. In this strategy, the aim is to stimulate B-cells [a type of immune cell] so that broadly protective antibodies are produced during influenza infection. The immune system naturally generates such antibodies, but they are rare—about one or two of the 10 000–100 000 antibodies generated during infection. "As yet", says McMichael, "we do not know how to make people make those antibodies rather than the ones which do not broadly protect, which vastly outnumber those that do."

In animal studies, some success has been reported recently with a vaccine composed of a relatively conserved haemagglutinin epitope bound to fragments of human immunoglobulin [antibody]. In mice, this recombinant fusion protein provided cross-protection against infection with divergent strains of highly pathogenic H5N1 virus. An alternative antigen focus is matrix protein 2—a surface glycoprotein that is more highly conserved than other coat proteins. An approach combining an inactivated vaccine (akin to that used for seasonal vaccination) and the matrix protein 2 contained in virus-like particles has proved successful at protecting mice against lethal challenge with several viruses, including the 2009 pandemic H1N1, and various strains of H5N1 and H3N2, the subtype that caused the Hong Kong influenza pandemic of 1968–69.

The other overarching strategy for new vaccine design aims to stimulate T-cell [a type of immune cell] responses that recognise the internal proteins of the virus, which are more highly conserved than coat proteins. Proteins such as matrix protein 1 and nucleoprotein are often very similar between emergent strains and seasonal strains, McMichael explains. "It is not clear yet in humans how much protection that kind of immune response offers", he says, but "a few experimental challenges of volunteers have suggested that these responses could be partially protective."

Shortly anticipated are the results of a phase 1 vaccine trial and experimental challenge, using a modified vaccinia virus Ankara to express matrix protein 1 and nucleoprotein. The study by Sarah Gilbert and co-workers at The Jenner Institute, University of Oxford, UK, is likely to shed light on the role of induced T-cell responses for influenza protection. McMichael told *TID* that vaccines that generate T-cell responses are more likely to lessen the effect of the infection than to stop infection altogether, so, ultimately, a combination of strategies might prove most effective, but that is some years away.

A Possible Preemptive Strategy

For now, a possible pre-emptive strategy is wide use of currently available vaccines—"universal" vaccination. For example, Gary Nabel and colleagues from the Vaccine Research Center of the US National Institutes of Health are advocating a pre-emptive vaccination programme for H2N2, a subtype linked to previous pandemics and currently circulating strains. The first step would be safety and efficacy testing of vaccines available from the Asian influenza pandemic of 1957–58, suggests Nabel.

However, emergent findings from the 2009 pandemic are reinforcing the concept that natural influenza infection is likely to induce broader and longer lasting immunity than that from killed vaccines. Self-limiting infection seems beneficial—"to 'fill in' our influenza immunity and provide us with an increased likelihood of cross-protection to a novel virus", explains Kelly. For this reason and others, he continues "it is argued that we should be cautious about recommendations for universal influenza vaccination—as opposed to a potential universal vaccine".

9

The World Health Organization Exaggerated the 2009 Swine Flu Pandemic

Michael Fumento

Michael Fumento is an investigative journalist, attorney, and author of several books. Specializing in health and science topics, his articles have appeared in magazines such as Readers' Digest, Atlantic Monthly, Forbes, Weekly Standard, National Review, Reason, *and others. His books include* The Myth of Heterosexual AIDS, Science Under Siege, *and* BioEvolution: How Biotechnology Is Changing Our World.

The 2009 swine flu "pandemic" was not a pandemic at all. Fewer people were killed in the so-called pandemic than die every year from the seasonal flu; however, the World Health Organization (WHO) needed a pandemic to restore their credibility. So the agency changed its official definition of pandemic to include mild outbreaks. This allowed the relatively mild swine flu outbreak of 2009 to be labeled a pandemic, but it really was not a pandemic. The WHO's exaggeration caused unnecessary fear and panic and wasted money that could have been spent battling other diseases.

Hallelujah, the disaster has been averted! The World Health Organization [WHO] last week [in August 2010] declared the H1N1 swine flu pandemic over.

Except for one little thing: It never happened. That is, the WHO had no business labeling it a "pandemic." It did so purely for its own interests, wreaking worldwide havoc.

In April 2009, WHO flu czar Keiji Fukuda declared that we could be facing a contagion on the order of the Spanish flu of 1918–19, and the United Nations soon concurred. Spanish flu killed about 50 million worldwide and 675,000 in the United States.

Yet, with the "pandemic" over, here's the final toll: "Over 18,449" people have died worldwide, says the WHO. By comparison, garden-variety seasonal flu normally kills 250,000 to 500,000 annually. The mildest pandemic of the 20th century killed a million people worldwide.

The WHO had no business labeling it a "pandemic." It did so purely for its own interests, wreaking worldwide havoc.

The U.S. had about 12,500 flu deaths, according to the Centers for Disease Control and Prevention (CDC), a third the usual number. Yet reported swine flu deaths in Canada were only about a tenth the usual rate, while the U.K. had an even lower ratio. That indicates the CDC figure is vastly too high.

So how does the WHO explain the fact that you're still alive to read this? We were "just plain lucky," shrugs Director-General Margaret Chan. That's really the best she could do—or felt she needed to do.

The WHO Wanted a Pandemic

In fact, there was never a need for luck or alarm. Just two days after Fukuda's Spanish flu comparison, I wrote of a "porcine panic." I went on to reiterate in many more articles that flu fears were being overblown: When the WHO made the pandemic official, for example, I noted that swine flu had killed only 144 people worldwide in 11 weeks, fewer than die *each day* from ordinary flu. If I knew the outbreak was being exaggerated, then the WHO and others knew or should have known.

The previous definition of influenza pandemic required "several, simultaneous epidemics worldwide with enormous numbers of deaths and illness." But the agency wanted an H1N1 pandemic—badly. It had lost credibility for sounding the alarm for five years about H5N1 avian flu described as a "when, not if" pandemic that could kill hundreds of millions.

So when swine flu trotted in, the WHO rewrote its definition to say pandemics "can be either mild or severe." That renders the term meaningless, because seasonal flu always causes "simultaneous epidemics worldwide."

This gave license to others to treat swine flu as a pandemic in the commonly accepted sense of the term. Thus, last August [2009], the President's Council of Advisors on Science and Technology forecast a "plausible" scenario of 30,000 to 90,000 U.S. deaths. In the *Washington Post*, author John Barry predicted more than 89,000 American deaths.

This was obviously nonsense. We already had information from all over the world showing swine flu to be vastly milder than the seasonal variety. A New York City estimate suggested that seasonal flu was 10 to 40 times deadlier than swine flu. In Australia, with the epidemic already well under way and no vaccine generally available, people were dying at a *lower* rate than normal.

Causing Panic, Wasting Money

In October, U.S. health officials launched a campaign to panic parents into getting their children inoculated, prompting such headlines as "CDC shocker: swine flu killing young people at record rate." This was inexcusably cruel: Not only were officials exaggerating a tiny risk; they were doing so when a vaccine wasn't widely available.

Today, with incredible chutzpah [boldness], the WHO even denies that it rewrote the definition of pandemic. "Having severe deaths has never been part of the WHO definition," Fukuda said. So what if references to the changed definition are all over the Web, including in the WHO archive? It's like Paris Hilton denying the existence of her sex tape.

Meanwhile, the world has wasted billions of dollars that could have been spent on diseases like tuberculosis, which each year kills 70 times as many people as swine flu did, according to the WHO. Now add in the "crying wolf" factor, which means many people will ignore public-health warnings when a truly nasty disease comes along, and you'll see how much damage was done by the swine flu disinformation campaign.

10

The World Health Organization Handled the 2009 Swine Flu Pandemic Well

World Health Organization

The World Health Organization (WHO) is the directing and co-ordinating authority for health within the United Nations system. It is responsible for providing leadership on global health matters, shaping the health research agenda, setting norms and standards, articulating evidence-based policy options, providing technical support to countries, and monitoring and assessing health trends.

Some in the media have questioned the World Health Organization's (WHO's) decision to label the 2009 H1N1 outbreak a pandemic and contend that it was unduly influenced by the pharmaceutical industry. This is not true. The WHO operates under numerous regulations that guard against conflicts of interest in its collaborations with pharmaceutical industry experts. The WHO had no hidden agenda in its decision to label the H1N1 outbreak a pandemic. It was managing the outbreak under the provisions of the revised International Health Regulations.

WHO [World Health Organization] is aware of some concerns, expressed in the media, that ties with the pharmaceutical industry among experts on the Organization's advisory bodies may influence policy decisions, especially those relating to the influenza pandemic.

World Health Organization, "WHO Use of Advisory Bodies in Responding to the Influenza Pandemic," World Health Organization, Global Alert and Response (GAR), December 3, 2009. http://www.who.int/csr/disease/swineflu/notes/briefing_20091203/en/index.html. Reproduced by permission of World Health Organization.

WHO has historically collaborated with the pharmaceutical industry for legitimate reasons. Efforts to improve health depend on better access to high-quality and affordable medicines, vaccines, and diagnostics. Medical interventions, including antiviral drugs, vaccines, and diagnostic tests, have long been recognized for their role in mitigating the health impact of an influenza pandemic. Pharmaceutical companies play an essential role in this regard and WHO has engaged with them to pursue its public health objectives.

Conflicts of Interest

Potential conflicts of interest are inherent in any relationship between a normative and health development agency, like WHO, and a profit-driven industry. Similar considerations apply when experts advising the Organization have professional links with pharmaceutical companies. Numerous safeguards are in place to manage possible conflicts of interest or their perception.

External experts who advise WHO are required to provide a declaration of interests that details professional or financial interests that could compromise the impartiality of their advice. Procedures are in place for identifying, investigating and assessing potential conflicts of interest, disclosing them, and taking appropriate action such as excluding an expert from participating in a meeting.

International Health Regulations

The influenza pandemic is providing the first major test of the revised International Health Regulations, which were approved by WHO Member States in 2005 and came into legal force in 2007. The Regulations provide an orderly, rules-based mechanism for coordinating the response to public health emergencies of international concern, such as that caused by the H1N1 pandemic virus.

Apart from protecting public health against the international spread of disease, the Regulations contain provisions for avoiding unnecessary interference with international travel and trade.

Under the provisions of the revised Regulations, an Emergency Committee advises the WHO Director-General on matters such as declaring a public health emergency of international concern, the need to raise the level of pandemic alert following spread of the H1N1 virus, and the need to introduce temporary measures, such as restrictions on travel or trade. Final decisions are made by the Director-General, as guided by the Committee's advice.

All members of the Emergency Committee sign a confidentiality agreement, provide a declaration of interests, and agree to give their consultative time freely, without compensation. Members of the Committee are drawn from a roster of about 160 experts covering a range of public health areas. The framework for membership is set out in the International Health Regulations. Each State Party to the Regulations is entitled to nominate one member of the roster and additional experts are appointed by the Director-General. Recommendations of the Emergency Committee are immediately made public on the WHO web site together with the relevant decisions of the Director-General.

The influenza pandemic is providing the first major test of the revised International Health Regulations, which were approved by WHO Member States in 2005.

Experts on Immunization

In responding to the pandemic, WHO has also drawn on advice from a standing body of experts, the Strategic Advisory Group of Experts on Immunization (SAGE), which advises WHO on vaccine use. Members of SAGE are likewise required to declare all professional and financial interests, including funding received from pharmaceutical companies or consultancies or other forms of professional engagement with pharmaceutical companies. The names and affiliations of members of SAGE and of SAGE working groups are published on the WHO web site, together with meeting reports and declarations of interest submitted by the experts.

Allegations of undeclared conflicts of interest are taken very seriously by WHO, and are immediately investigated.

Unfounded Criticisms

Public perceptions about the [2009] H1N1 influenza pandemic, as well as national preparedness plans, were strongly influenced by a five-year close watch over the highly lethal H5N1 avian influenza virus, which was widely regarded as the virus most likely to ignite the next influenza pandemic. A pandemic caused by a virus that kills more than 60% of the people it infects is strikingly, and fortunately, very different from the reality of the [2009] pandemic.

Adjusting public perceptions to suit a far less lethal virus has been problematic. Given the discrepancy between what was expected and what has happened, a search for ulterior motives on the part of WHO and its scientific advisers is understandable, though without justification.

WHO has consistently assessed the impact of the current influenza pandemic as moderate. WHO has consistently reminded the medical community, public, and media that the overwhelming majority of patients experience mild influenza-like illness and recover fully within a week, even without any form of medical treatment. WHO has consistently advised against any restrictions on travel or trade. Although influenza viruses are notoriously unpredictable, it is hoped that this moderate impact will continue throughout the duration of the pandemic.

11

Another Pandemic Is Inevitable

John M. Barry

John M. Barry is an author and policy adviser. His articles have appeared in innumerable scientific and nonscientific journals. He is the author of The Great Influenza, *a study of the 1918 pandemic, which was named a National Academy of Sciences outstanding book on science or medicine. Barry has advised the administrations of George W. Bush and Barack Obama and worked with the World Health Organization on pandemic response.*

There will be more flu pandemics in the future, and no one can predict how lethal they will be. The 1918 flu pandemic killed 60 percent of those infected, while the 2009 flu pandemic killed only tens of thousands worldwide. The world is lucky that the 2009 pandemic was mild, because the international community's response to the pandemic was flawed. Some countries, including the United States, acted in their own self-interest, while other countries, such as China, acted irrationally and even lied about the facts. The global pandemic response must improve, because there will inevitably be another pandemic.

It is the nature of the influenza virus to cause pandemics. There have been at least 11 in the last 300 years, and there will certainly be another one, and one after that, and another after that. And it is impossible to predict whether a pandemic will be mild or lethal.

In 1997 in Hong Kong, the H5N1 virus jumped directly from chickens to 18 people, killing six. Public health officials

John M. Barry, "The Next Pandemic," *World Policy Journal*, Summer 2010. Copyright © 2010 World Policy Institute. Reproduced by permission.

slaughtered hundreds of thousands of ducks, chickens and other fowl to prevent further spread, and the virus seemed contained. It wasn't. In 2004, H5N1 returned with a vengeance. Since then, it has killed hundreds of millions of birds, while several hundred million more have been culled in prevention efforts. And it has infected more than 500 human beings, killing 60 percent of those infected. The virus's high mortality rate and memories of the 1918 influenza—the best estimates of that death toll range from 35 to 100 million people—got the world's attention. Every developed nation prepared for a pandemic, as did local and regional governments and the private sector. They all based their preparations on a 1918-like scenario, but it did not come. It still could.

In March 2009, another influenza pandemic caused by a different virus did arrive, and it was nothing like the lethal one we expected. This particular H1N1 virus generated a pandemic with the lowest case mortality rate of any known outbreak in history. Nothing the world did accounted for the low death toll; it was simply luck that this pandemic virus had low lethality. The World Health Organization [WHO] counts fewer than 20,000 dead worldwide, but that's only laboratory-confirmed cases. It is impossible to know whether actual mortality was 10 or even 100 times that number.

There have been at least 11 [pandemics] in the last 300 years, and there will certainly be another one, and one after that, and another after that.

But even the highest reasonable estimate of those killed by this latest pandemic so far—we could still see more waves of infection—still falls far below the anticipated scenario. The world assumed that preparing for a severe pandemic would allow it to adjust easily to a mild one. It was mistaken. This lesser pandemic threw the world off-balance, and very few nations have, with respect to influenza, regained their footing.

A World Under Pressure

The 2009 pandemic put the world under pressure and revealed flaws in both health systems and, more significantly, in international relations. The lessons we might learn from this past event could be of value in our ongoing war against the flu virus. But we're still getting too many things wrong.

Virologists, epidemiologists, public health officials, even ethicists and logisticians are analyzing data from the pandemic. Based on their results, health organizations will likely adopt modest management changes. The WHO previously defined an influenza pandemic as basically any occurrence in which a new influenza virus enters the human population and passes easily between humans; it may refine that definition by adding a virulence factor, similar to the Saffir-Simpson scale for hurricanes (category 1 to category 5). Vaccine delivery systems will improve. Local hospitals will upgrade their triage practices. And some fundamental changes which were already under way—such as shifting vaccine production away from chicken eggs, a technology used for more than half a century, to new production technologies—will accelerate.

These are good starting points. But on larger policy and scientific questions any efforts to draw conclusions could mislead. All other pandemics we know about in any detail—in 1918, 1957 and 1968—sickened 25 percent of the population or more in every country for which data exists. The 2009 data suggests attack rates approached that benchmark figure in children only, while adults were generally attacked at only a quarter to a half that rate, not because of any public health measures taken but most likely because adults had already been exposed to a similar virus and had some immunity. This distinctly unusual pattern makes it difficult to draw conclusions on the effectiveness of, for example, such non-pharmaceutical interventions as screening airport arrivals or shutting down schools. Yet some epidemiologists are insisting on doing just that. Policy for the next pandemic is being set, and it is based on the analysis of *sui generis* [unique] data.

The world needs to learn the right political lessons, too, and so far it has shown no sign of doing so. Instead, a scapegoat is being groomed. The WHO has come under intense attack for declaring a pandemic at all, and critics have even charged the pharmaceutical industry with influencing the decision. This is nonsense. The spring of 1918 saw a mild initial flu much like 2009—so mild, in fact, that the British Grand Fleet patrolling Europe's coast had 10,313 sailors sick enough to miss duty during war, but only four died. Yet several months later, Armageddon arrived. Aware of that history, the WHO was all but compelled to act as it did. If the current criticism of the WHO makes it more cautious in the future, the world will become a more dangerous place.

The real overreaction came not from the WHO but from the nations that ignored the accurate epidemiological and clinical information the WHO regularly released. These countries refused to adjust their response and implemented extreme measures, either out of irrational fears or for domestic political reasons.

Mexico Punished for Honesty

The world needs transparency about disease. Mexico, where H1N1 first appeared in humans, told the truth, and for this it was roundly punished. Since there was no possibility of containing the virus, WHO and FAO [United Nations Food and Agriculture Organization] explicitly recommended against trade or travel restrictions. Yet at least 25 countries limited trade with or travel to Mexico. France demanded that the EU [European Union] suspend all flights there, and although that did not happen, the EU and the U.S. government recommended canceling non-essential travel to Mexico—although the U.S. soon had more cases of H1N1. The World Bank estimated that this mild pandemic cost the Mexican economy 0.7

percent of GDP [gross domestic product]. Such political reaction makes the world less safe, since it makes countries less likely to tell the truth for fear of the repercussions.

Even more disturbing, a host of nations revealed themselves as determinedly and self-destructively committed to their individual political interests. It should surprise no one that the United States promised last September [2009] to give some vaccine to countries without any, then retracted the promise when production lagged, saying it first had to protect its own vulnerable population. But breaking a commitment sets a dangerous precedent—the United States imports almost 70 percent of its vaccine. In a severe pandemic, political leaders of an exporting country could refuse to allow their manufacturers to ship supplies to the United States until its own population is protected, and cite this U.S. precedent.

National Irrationality

At least hoarding vaccine to protect your domestic population is rational. The pandemic also demonstrated the irrationality of nations. Egypt exploited the outbreak to slaughter all pigs, a popular act since Muslims don't eat pork. Several countries either lied or all but totally misunderstood the threat. Indonesia's health minister told his citizens they had no need to worry about H1N1 because they lived in a tropical climate. Chinese Health Minister Chen Zhu initially declared, "We are confident and capable of preventing and containing an H1N1 influenza epidemic." Yet this is, literally, impossible. In late September, with H1N1 already throughout China, he said his country would focus its vaccine effort on areas with the greatest interaction with foreigners since it remained "a foreign disease."

Such actions neither encourage nor reflect transparency, and destroy trust between nations. They are counterproductive domestically, undermining a government's credibility. Above all, they too make the world a more dangerous place.

In 2009 the world in effect took a test. At the scientific and technocratic levels, it did reasonably well. But at the level where politicians operate, too many countries failed, and failed miserably. That does not portend well for the future.

Everything that happened in 2009 suggests that, if a severe outbreak comes again, failure to improve on our response will threaten chaos and magnify the terror, the economic impact and the death toll. And it will come again.

The H5N1 virus continues to infect and kill. It's still a threat as a pandemic, while HIV and SARS [severe acute respiratory syndrome] demonstrate that new infectious diseases can emerge at any time. Meanwhile, a sense of complacency seems to be settling over the world. Because H5N1 has not become pandemic and H1N1 turned out to be mild, the idea that influenza is no longer a threat has become pervasive. Everything that happened in 2009 suggests that, if a severe outbreak comes again, failure to improve on our response will threaten chaos and magnify the terror, the economic impact and the death toll. And it will come again.

Organizations to Contact

The editors have compiled the following list of organizations concerned with the issues debated in this book. The descriptions are derived from materials provided by the organizations. All have publications or information available for interested readers. The list was compiled on the date of publication of the present volume; the information provided here may change. Be aware that many organizations take several weeks or longer to respond to inquiries, so allow as much time as possible.

American Public Health Association (APHA)
800 Eye St. NW, Washington, DC   20001
(202) 777-2742 • fax: (202) 777-2534
e-mail: comments@apha.org
website: www.apha.org

The American Public Health Association is a professional organization for public health professionals in the United States. The APHA's mission is to protect all Americans and their communities from preventable, serious health threats, and it strives to ensure that community-based health promotion and disease prevention activities and preventative health services are universally accessible in the United States. The APHA publishes the monthly *American Journal of Public Health*, and various reports, issue briefs, and fact sheets are available on the organization's website.

Center for Biosecurity of University of Pittsburgh Medical Center
The Pier IV Bldg., 621 E. Pratt St., Suite 210
Baltimore, MD   21202
(443) 573-3304 • fax: (443) 573-3305
website: www.upmc-biosecurity.org

The Center for Biosecurity of University of Pittsburgh Medical Center is an independent nonprofit organization. The center works to affect policy and practice in ways that lessen the illness, death, and civil disruption that would follow large-scale epidemics, whether they occur naturally or result from the use of a biological weapon. The Center for Biosecurity Network (CBN) is a secure website run by the center that provides authoritative and timely information to clinicians who are interested in biodefense preparedness and response. The *CBN Report* provides brief summaries describing recent developments in science, public health, medicine, governance, national/homeland security, and domestic/foreign policy that have significance for clinicians involved in biodefense. The *CBN Special Bulletin* publishes up-to-date information during times of unusual and/or ongoing circumstances, such as suspected or confirmed bioterrorism attacks, emergent disease outbreaks, or when there are other threats to the nation's medical and/or public health systems.

Center for Infectious Disease Research and Policy (CIDRAP)

University of Minnesota, Academic Health Center
420 Delaware St. SE, MMC 263, Minneapolis, MN   55455
(612) 626-6770 • fax: (612) 626-6783
e-mail: cidrap@umn.edu
website: www.cidrap.umn.edu

The mission of the Center for Infectious Disease Research and Policy, which is part of the Academic Health Center at the University of Minnesota, is to reduce global illness and death from infectious diseases. CIDRAP focuses its efforts on pandemic influenza preparedness, bioterrorism preparedness, and other emerging or potential global health challenges. The center fulfills its mission through education, consensus building, and conducting original research. CIDRAP is involved in several pandemic preparedness initiatives and programs, including the Minnesota Center of Excellence for Influenza Research and Surveillance (MCEIRS), the CIDRAP Comprehensive Influenza Vaccine Initiative, and the BioWatch air-monitoring program. The CIDRAP website provides current, in-depth information, news stories, reports, and articles on bioterrorism, influenza, and emerging infectious diseases.

Centers for Disease Control and Prevention (CDC)

Office of Public Health Preparedness and Response
1600 Clifton Rd., Atlanta, GA   30333
(800) 232-4636
e-mail: cdcinfo@cdc.gov
website: www.cdc.gov/phpr

The primary mission of the Centers for Disease Control and Prevention, an agency under the US Department of Health and Human Services, is to protect public health and safety. The Office of Public Health Preparedness and Response (PHPR) within the CDC leads the agency's preparedness and response activities to pandemics and other public health emergencies by providing strategic direction, support, and coordination for activities across the CDC as well as with local, state, tribal, national, territorial, and international public health partners. The PHPR website provides information on public health threats, statistics on state emergency health preparedness planning, and a public health blog.

CORE Group

100 G St. NW, Suite 400, Washington, DC   20005
(202) 380-3400
e-mail: contact@coregroupdc.org
website: www.coregroup.org

CORE Group is an organization of health professionals from nongovernmental development organizations committed to sharing knowledge and ideas about how to best help children survive. The CORE Group vision is "a world of healthy communities, where no woman or child dies of preventable causes." The CORE Group is part of the Humanitarian Pandemic Preparedness (H2P) Initiative (www.pandemicprepared ness.org) along with partners, including the International Federation of Red Cross and Red Crescent Societies, the Academy for Educational Development, InterAction, and the United Nations. The overall goal of H2P is to build humanitarian response networks and ready-to-use tools to enable community-level response to a pandemic event. The CORE Group website provides planning tools for communities, working papers, case studies, and online tutorials.

Infectious Diseases Society of America (IDSA)
1300 Wilson Blvd., Suite 300, Arlington, VA   22209
(703) 299-0200 • fax: (703) 299-0204
website: www.idsociety.org

The Infectious Diseases Society of America is an organization of physicians, scientists, and health care professionals who specialize in infectious diseases. IDSA's purpose is to improve the health of individuals, communities, and society by promoting excellence in patient care, education, research, public health, and prevention relating to infectious diseases. Among its activities, IDSA works as an advocacy group to promote sound public policy on infectious diseases. One concern of the society is pandemic influenza. IDSA seeks to promote a science-based and effective government pandemic response. The society offers several publications, including *IDSA News*, the *Journal of Clinical Infectious Diseases*, and the *Journal of Infectious Diseases*.

Robert Wood Johnson Foundation (RWJF)
PO Box 2316, Route 1 and College Rd. East
Princeton, NJ   08543-2316
(877) 843-7953
website: www.rwjf.org

The mission of the Robert Wood Johnson Foundation is to improve the health and health care of all Americans. As part of its mission, the foundation works to strengthen US preparedness for future potential flu outbreaks and other national health emergencies. The RWJF sponsors pandemic preparedness symposiums, develops tool kits to help local community health officials prepare for pandemics, and sponsors research to help learn what works best in pandemic preparedness. The foundation's website provides issue briefs, reports, and articles, as well as blogs on public health and pandemic preparedness.

Trust for America's Health (TFAH)

1730 M St. NW, Suite 900, Washington, DC   20036
(202) 223-9870 • fax: (202) 223-9871
e-mail: info@tfah.org
website: www.healthyamericans.org

Trust for America's Health is a nonprofit, nonpartisan organization dedicated to saving lives by protecting the health of every community and working to make disease prevention a national priority. TFAH's pandemic initiative focuses on prevention, protection, and communities. The organization works to educate policy makers on ways to better prepare the country for a possible pandemic outbreak. The organization has issued a series of reports and brochures for families, medical providers, businesses, and community leaders who want to learn more about how to prepare for a possible pandemic.

US Agency for International Development (USAID)

Ronald Reagan Bldg., Washington, DC   20523-1000
(202) 712-4810 • fax: (202) 216-3524
website: www.usaid.gov

The US Agency for International Development is an international aid agency of the US government. The USAID works in one hundred developing countries providing disaster relief, aiding the effort to end poverty, and helping to promote democratic reforms. USAID programs in global health address disease prevention and management. Some of the major diseases addressed by USAID include HIV/AIDS, malaria, and avian influenza. USAID provides funding to help fight these pandemics worldwide. The USAID website provides a searchable database of case studies and reports on the agency's work, as well as many fact sheets and other publications.

World Health Organization (WHO)
Global Influenza Programme

Avenue Appia 20, Geneva 27   1211
  Switzerland
+41 22 791 21 11 • fax: +41 22 791 31 11

e-mail: info@who.int
website: www.who.int

The World Health Organization is the directing and coordinating authority for health within the United Nations system. It is responsible for providing leadership on global health matters, shaping the health research agenda, setting norms and standards, articulating evidence-based policy options, providing technical support to countries, and monitoring and assessing health trends. The WHO facilitates pandemic preparedness around the world by providing influenza surveillance, facilitating the exchange of information between countries, and helping to increase vaccine supplies and ensure their equitable distribution.

Bibliography

Books

Jon Stuart Abramson — *Inside the 2009 Influenza Pandemic.* Hackensack, NJ: World Scientific, 2011.

John Barry — *The Great Influenza: The Story of the Deadliest Pandemic in History.* New York: Penguin, 2005.

Richard Compans and Walter Orenstein — *Vaccines for Pandemic Influenza.* New York: Springer, 2009.

Mark Honigsbaum — *Living with Enza: The Forgotten Story of Britain and the Great Flu Pandemic of 1918.* New York: Macmillan, 2009.

Institute of Medicine — *Antivirals for Pandemic Influenza: Guidance on Developing a Distribution and Dispensing Program.* Washington, DC: National Academies Press, 2007.

Paul Kupperberg — *The Influenza Pandemic of 1918–1919.* New York: Chelsea House, 2008.

Lester Little — *Plague and the End of Antiquity: The Pandemic of 541–750.* New York: Cambridge University Press, 2007.

William Long — *Pandemics and Peace: Public Health Cooperation in Zones of Conflict.* Washington, DC: US Institute of Peace Press, 2011.

Christopher Mari	*Global Epidemics.* New York: H.W. Wilson, 2007.
Paul Offit	*Vaccinated: One Man's Quest to Defeat the World's Deadliest Diseases.* Washington, DC: Smithsonian Books, 2007.
Dorothy Pettit	*A Cruel Wind: Pandemic Flu in America 1918–1920.* Murfreesboro, TN: Timberlane Books, 2008.
Gary Ridenour	*Pandemic.* Reno, NV: Jack Bacon, 2007.
Alan Sipress	*The Fatal Strain: On the Trail of Avian Flu and the Coming Pandemic.* New York: Viking, 2009.
Lauren Sompayrac	*How Pathogenic Viruses Work.* Sudbury, MA: Jones & Bartlett, 2002.

Periodicals and Internet Sources

Amesh Adalja	"Redefining Influenza 'Pandemic,'" *CBN Report*, May 20, 2011.
Scott Allen	"Scientists Re-create 1918 Flu Pandemic Virus," *Boston Globe*, October 6, 2005.
Nicholas Bakalar	"What's a Little Swine Flu Outbreak Among Friends?" *New York Times*, February 3, 2011.
Carol Baker	"Flu Vaccination: Adopt '3-R' Approach," *Pediatric News*, January 2011.

Tamar Ben-Yedidia	"Progress Towards a Universal Influenza Vaccine," *Future Virology*, February 2011.
Corey Binns	"Predicting Pandemics," *Popular Science*, June, 2008.
Economist	"How Dr Chan Intends to Defend the Planet from Pandemics," June 16, 2007.
Antoine Flahault and Patrick Zylberman	Influenza Pandemics: Past, Present and Future Challenges, *Public Health Reviews*, 2010.
Katherine Harris, Jürgen Maurer, and Arthur Kellermann	"Influenza Vaccine—Safe, Effective, and Mistrusted," *New England Journal of Medicine*, November 24, 2010.
Tom Junod	"Why There Won't Be a Deadly Flu Pandemic," *Esquire*, December 2005.
Jeffrey Levi, Thomas Inglesby, Laura Segal, and Serena Vinter	"Pandemic Flu Preparedness: Lessons from the Frontlines," Robert Wood Johnson Foundation, Trust for America's Health, and the Center for Biosecurity of the University of Pittsburgh Medical Center, June 2009.
Mike McGuire	"Our Pandemic Disconnect," *Occupational Health & Safety*, November 2008.
MedicalCare.org	"H1N1 Swine Flu Triggers Super Immunity," January 17, 2011. www.medicalcare.org.

Newsweek	"Fear & the Flu: The New Age of Pandemics," May 25, 2009.
John Oxford	"Viewpoint—Influenza A H1N1: Past and Future," *GP*, March 10, 2011.
Cindy Patton	"Pandemic, Empire and the Permanent State of Exception," *Economic & Political Weekly*, March 26, 2011.
Timothy Renick	"Be Very Afraid: The Cultural Response to Terror, Pandemics, Environmental Devastation, Nuclear Annihilation, and Other Threats," *Christian Century*, June 1, 2010.
Tina Hesman Saey	"H1N1 Exploited Antibody Mismatch: Middle-Aged Flu Victims May Have Succumbed to Friendly Fire," ScienceNews.com, January 1, 2011. www.sciencenews.com.
Monica Schoch-Spana and Ann Norwood	"Stigma: Its Harm and Its Remedy in Outbreaks Like Swine Flu," *Center for Biosecurity: Swine Flu Issue Brief*, April 29, 2009.
Marilyn Werber Serafini, Randy Barrett, and Munro Neil	"U.S. Remains Unready for Pandemic," *National Journal*, May 8, 2009.
Space Daily	"Bacteria Seek to Topple the Egg as Top Flu Vaccine Tool," December 13, 2010.

US Department of Health and Human Services   "The Great Pandemic: United States in 1918–1919." http://1918.pandemic flu.gov.

Bryan Walsh et al.   "A Wing and a Prayer," *Time*, September 26, 2005.

Index

Numerals

1918–1919 influenza pandemic
    death from, 23, 53
    face mask laws, 26–27
    mandatory NPI, 25
    memory of, 82

A

Accountability principle, of preparedness, 20
Adjuvants in flu vaccines, 45
Advance Market Commitments for Vaccines, 63
Africa, 51
Algorithm evaluation, 36
Annas, George J., 16–21
Anti-vaccine hype, 46–48
Antibiotic resistance, 31
Antibody response, 69–70
Asia, 13–14
Attkisson, Sharyl, 44
Australia
    flu vaccines, 12, 59, 68
    Swine flu in, 75
Avian "bird" flu (H5N1)
    antibody response, 70
    controversies over, 58–59
    costs of, 31
    death from, 44, 68
    egg process, 13
    fears of, 16
    impact of, 80, 81–82, 86
    preparation for, 40, 42
    vaccines for, 57–58, 69

B

Barry, John M., 75, 81–86
Bill and Melinda Gates Foundation, 42, 54
Biological and Toxin Weapons Convention, 33
Biological disasters, 18
Biological research, 38
Biosurveillance and reporting, 35–37
Bird flu. *See* Avian "bird" flu
Borlaug, Norman, 32
Branswell, Helen, 40, 42–43
Bush, George W., 18

C

Campaign for Access to Essential Medicines, 63
Canada
    avian "bird" flu, 59
    flu vaccines, 12, 46
Canadian Press, 40, 42
Cell-based vaccines, 13–14
Centers for Disease Control and Prevention (CDC), 24, 44, 74–75
Chan, Margaret, 52–53, 74
Chen Zhu, 85
China, 85
Clinton Global Initiative, 63
Compacts against pandemic threat, 33–38
Consultative Group on International Agricultural Research (CGIAR), 32

Containment strategy, 19

Conventions against pandemic threat, 33

Council on Foreign Relations (CFR)

globalism and, 39–41, 45–46, 48–49

humanitarian solutions, 49–51

medical crises and, 43

CSL Limited, 7–9, 12

D

Department of Health and Human Services (DHHS)

cell-based vaccine facilities, 13

pandemic preparedness, 19

vaccine distribution and, 8–9

Department of Homeland Security (DHS), 8–9

Doctors Without Borders, 63

E

Emanuel, Ezekiel J., 9

Epidemiologists, 83–84

Equitable access to vaccines, 60–64

Ethical concerns

nonpharmaceutical intervention, 23–27

pandemic preparedness, 27–29, 83

vaccine distribution, 8–9

European Union, 40, 84

F

Face mask laws, 26–27

"False pandemics," 66

Fear mongering, 44–46

Fidler, David P., 57–66

Financial Times, 41

Flu strains, 7–8, 43

See also specific flu strains

Flu vaccines. *See* Pandemic flu vaccines; Seasonal flu vaccines

Food and Agriculture Organization (FAO), 84

Food and Drug Administration (FDA)

medically-caused deaths, 50

vaccine testing, 12–13

Forcible vaccination, 17

Fuego, Tierra Del, 42

Fukuda, Keiji, 60, 74, 75

Fumento, Michael, 73–76

G

Garrett, Laurie, 40, 41–42

Gilbert, Sarah, 71

GlaxoSmithKline, 12, 53–55

Global access framework, 60

Global Alliance for Vaccines and Immunisation (GAVI), 63

Global food crisis, 32

Global Influenza Surveillance Network, 58

Globalism, 39–41, 45–46, 48–49

Gottlieb, Scott, 11–15

H

Haemagglutinin epitope, 70

Harvard School of Public Health survey, 24

Health principle of preparedness, 19

Hepatitis B, 54

Hoarding flu vaccines, 85

Hong Kong influenza pandemic, 70

Human immunoglobulin, 70

Humanitarian solutions, 48–51

I

Immunization experts, 79–80

Indonesia, "viral sovereignty," 64

Infectious diseases, 30, 34

Information technology (IT), 35–36

Intergovernmental Meeting (IGM), 60

International Campaign to Ban Landmines (ICBL), 31–32

International Compact for Infectious Diseases, 34–38

International Finance Facility for Immunization, 63

International Health Regulations (WHO), 35, 78–79

International pandemic response
anti-vaccine hype, 46–48
fear mongering, 44–46
humanitarian solutions, 48–51
medical crises and, 41–43
national sovereignty and, 42–43
overview, 39–41

International Seabed Authority, 63

J

Jack, Andrew, 41

Johns Hopkins School of Public Health, 50

Journal of the American Medical Association, 50

Justice principle of preparedness, 19

K

Kelly, Heath, 68–69

L

"Lab to jab" time, 66

Lancet, 9

Lange, John, 42

Lifecycle-allocation principle, 9

M

Mandatory nonpharmaceutical interventions
case for, 25–26
challenges with, 26–27
voluntary NPI *vs.,* 23–25

Mariner, Wendy K., 16–21

Markel, Howard, 22–30

McMichael, Andrew, 68–71

Measles, 54

Medical crises, 41–43

Mexico, H1N1 virus, 84–85

Microbial Threats of the Institute of Medicine, 60

Microbiologists, 34

Morris, Kelly, 67–72

N

Nabel, Gary, 71

National Institutes of Health, 71

National security issues, 12, 15, 20–21

National sovereignty, 42–43

Natural disasters, 18

Nongovernmental organizations (NGOs), 31–32, 36
Nonpharmaceutical interventions (NPI), 18, 23–25, 29
    See also Mandatory nonpharmaceutical interventions
Novartis, 13, 53
Nuclear disasters, 18

O

Obama, Barack, 11–12, 45–46

P

Pan-influenza (universal) vaccine. *See* Universal flu vaccine
Pandemic flu vaccines
    adjuvants in, 45
    availability of, 7–9, 38, 52–57
    cell-based vaccines, 13–14
    death from, 9
    distribution of, 8–9, 26
    donations of, 45–46, 54, 61–62
    forcible vaccination, 17
    immunization experts, 79–80
    overview, 57–58
    production of, 34–35, 65–66
    purchased, 13–14
    seasonal *vs.*, 8
    stockpiling, 20
    toxicity of, 46
    See also Universal flu vaccine
Pandemic flu vaccines, equitable access
    challenges to, 64–66
    controversy over, 58–59
    global access network, 60
    hoarding, 85
    International law, 62–64
    negotiating, 60–62
    overview, 57–58
Pandemic Influenza: Science, Economics, and Foreign Policy, 40
Pandemic Influenza Plan (DHHS), 19
Pandemic preparedness
    ethical concerns over, 27–29
    new paradigm for, 19–21
    overview, 11–12, 16–17
    post 9/11, 18–19
    quarantine measures and, 22–29
    vaccine capacity, 13–15
    vaccine shortages, 12–13
    See also International pandemic response; Nonpharmaceutical interventions
Pandemic Severity Index, 24
Pandemic threat
    biosurveillance and reporting, 35–37
    compacts, 33–38
    containment strategy, 19
    defined, 44, 75
    global effort against, 31–32
    as inevitable, 81–86
    peak attack rate, 26
    therapeutics for, 38
    treaties and conventions, 33
Parmet, Wendy E., 16–21
Pathologists, 34
Peak attack rate, 26
Persad, Govind, 9
Pharmaceutical companies, 37
Polio, 54
President's Council of Advisors on Science and Technology, 75
President's Emergency Plan for AIDS Relief, 62

Public health policy, 16–18
Purchased vaccine, 13–14

Q

Quarantine measures
  disease spread and, 17–20
  at home, 24
  pandemic preparedness and, 22–29
  voluntary, 26

R

Rao, C. Kameswara, 30–38
Rappoport, Jon, 39–51
Rationing schemes, 20
Recombinant technologies, 14
Regulatory agencies, 55–56
Rubin, Harvey, 30–38, 34
Rubin, Robert, 41

S

Saffir-Simpson scale, 83
Sanofi-Aventis, 12, 53–55
Sciences research centers, 34
Seasonal flu vaccines
  cost of, 53
  pandemic *vs.*, 8
  purchase of, 13–14
  vaccines for, 68
Sebelius, Kathleen, 59
Self-limiting infection, 71
Severe Acute Respiratory Syndrome (SARS)
  cost of, 31
  death from, 44
  fears over, 48
  lessons from, 23–24
Spanish flu, 74

Squalene, defined, 45
Standard Material Transfer Agreement (SMTA), 60, 61
Stern, Alexandra Minna, 22–30
Stockpiling vaccines, 20
Strategic Advisory Group of Experts on Immunization (SAGE), 79–80
Sui generis (unique) data, 84
Swine flu (H1N1)
  antibody response, 69–70
  death from, 44, 74
  donation of, 45–46
  exaggeration of, 73–76
  fear mongering, 44–45, 49
  globalism and, 40–41
  lessons from, 11–13, 42
  Mexico and, 84–85
  panic over, 75–76
  status of, 52–53
  vaccine hoarding, 85
  vaccines for, 57–58, 68
  WHO handling of, 77–80, 82

T

T-cell responses, 70–71
Transparency principle of preparedness, 19
Treaties against pandemic threat, 33

U

UN Convention on the Law of the Sea (UNCLOS), 63
United Nations (UN), 48, 59, 74, 84
United States (U.S.), flu vaccine
  donation of, 85
  increasing capacity, 13–15

medical-care system, 50
public health policy, 16–18
SARS costs, 31
shortage of, 12–13
Universal flu vaccine
appeal of, 68–69
overview, 67
preemptive strategies, 71–72
production strategies, 69–71

V

Vaccine Research Center, 71
Victorian Infectious Diseases Reference Laboratory, 68
Vietnam, 13
"Viral sovereignty," 64
Virologists, 83
Viruslike particles, 14
Voluntary nonpharmaceutical interventions, 18, 23–25, 29

W

Washington Post, 75
Weatherall Institute of Molecular Medicine, 68

Wertheimer, Alan, 9
West Nile virus, 44
Wilson, Patrick, 69
World Health Organization (WHO)
avian "bird" flu (H5N1), 58
benefit sharing, 60
Constitution, 62
criticisms of, 80
"false pandemics," 66
flu strains and, 7–8
humanitarian solutions, 48–49, 56
International Health Regulations, 35, 78–79
pandemic, defined, 44, 75
power of, 42
Swine Flu, exaggeration by, 73–77
Swine Flu, handling of, 77–80, 82
travel restrictions by, 84
vaccine development, 61
vaccine toxicity, 46

Y

Yamada, Tadataka, 52–56